A Treasury of Successful Appeal Letters

A TREASURY OF SUCCESSFUL APPEAL LETTERS

Edited by Joseph Dermer

Public Service Materials Center

111 N. Central Avenue
Hartsdale, New York 10530

ISBN: 0-914977-07-5

Library of Congress Catalog Card No. 85-60 108

Printed in the United States of America
10 9 8 7 6 5 4 3 2 1

Contents

Foreword

This collection of America's most successful fund raising letters is the second such book published by Public Service Materials Center. The first was published in 1976. This edition is larger, contains more letters—and also a wholly new feature. When an additional element was integral to the success of the letter, be it an unusual response device or enclosure, or even the mailing envelope itself—we have reproduced this element along with the letter.

On the adjoining page is our own letter which was sent to well over 100,000 members of the fund raising community. The response was impressive—far more letters and commentaries than we could hope to publish. However, with many hundreds of letters to choose from, we were able to strike a balance that we believe will be particularly helpful to the wide variety of fund raising people who will read this book.

Thus, you will find letters as long as four pages and as brief as two or three paragraphs. Virtually every kind of non-profit organization from giant universities to small community agencies, from leading hospitals to local humane societies is respresented in the pages that follow.

While most of the letters ask for money, there are others that do no more than say thank you in an unusually memorable fashion. Still others ask for pieces of equipment or seek to increase membership or are aimed at cultivating a relationship, or, in at least one instance, attempt to inform fellow employees what a development office is all about.

All of the letters have one thing in common. They were successful, many spectacularly so. You will, of course, read the letters, but study the commentaries as well. Taken as a group, they represent as good a practical guide to the art of writing successful appeal letters as exists today.

A final word. As you will note, there are three top award winners. The letters are all good, obviously. Some are quite stunning. So the selection of the three best was anything but an easy undertaking. To save you time in searching out the winners, they appear on the following pages:

First Prize: 9

Second Prize: 131

Third Prize: 52

PUBLIC SERVICE MATERIALS CENTER, INC.
111 N. Central Ave. • Hartsdale, N.Y. 10530 • (914) 949-2242

Dear Colleague:

Here is a chance to win fame, fortune (albeit, a modest one) and the admiration of your confreres.

Public Service Materials Center is interested in publishing the direct mail letter that you consider to be the best you have ever created -- be it for a contribution, renewal of a gift, bequest, membership, volunteer enlistment, alumni support, thank you or what have you.

Together with the letter, we want to publish up to 200 of your words telling why you think the letter is so good, including results obtained. To qualify, entries must be postmarked no later than Monday, October 15, 1984.

We will award prizes:

- $350 for letter and commentary we think best
- $200 for second best
- $100 for third best
- And $25 if we publish your letter and commentary at all.

You will also receive, of course, a complimentary copy of the book in which your material is published.

Do let us hear from you. It will take just a little bit of your time. It will be fun, and it will add some topflight professional literature to our field.

Sincerely,

Sylvia Shaw
Administrative Director

P.S. In the meanwhile, we suggest that you look over the enclosed Catalogue and leaflets for information about books that may help your fund raising.

Social Welfare Agencies

Carbon Copy Helps Raise $4.56 Per Dollar Spent

Our direct mail campaign is very much in its infancy and very new to our mailing list. Our agency has never before had a direct mail campaign, prior to 1983, and therefore we have many "first letters."

The total dollars raised may not seem remarkable on the surface; however, when one considers that the individuals who received the letter were not used to giving money to this agency at all, the dollars become most significant.

The material that follows contains two separate documents:

1. The original letter.

2. A hand written note that accompanied a carbon copy of the original letter.

The original and the carbon copy are printed, in house, by a letter quality printer at the same time. The original is mailed, of course, to all mailing list individuals and the carbon copy is mailed four weeks later to only those individuals who did not give to the original letter. It is most interesting to note, consistently, for all of our letters, over half of the total contributions come from the carbon copy.

Also in the material that follows is our "thank you" letter. It was sent with a pocket calendar with our logo and motto so that the donors would think of us throughout the year. The calendars were very well accepted and we received a number of thank yous from the donors.

Our Christmas letter was our most impressive for the following reasons:

1. Total contributions $24,370.00

   a. Original letter 9,133.00

   b. Carbon copy 15,237.00

(This letter also jogged the memory of a number of our donors to the Capital Campaign program and resulted in approximately $6,000 of pledges.)

2. This is our first Christmas letter.

3. The artwork was donated.

4. Total donors—759

   a. 63.5% of the donors were new for the year.

   b. 17.4% of the donors were giving their first gift in their donor history.

   c. This is a 63% increase in donors from our best letter prior to this time.

5. The average gift was $32.11.

6. The return was 10.7%.

7. The return for dollar spent in expenses was $4.56.

We are very pleased, as you can see, with this first Christmas letter and hope that you will share our enthusiasm.

Dan J. Pennell, M.S.W.

Editor's Note: We do, indeed. This entry was awarded First Prize.

GOLDIE B. FLOBERG CENTER FOR CHILDREN
58 WEST ROCKTON ROAD ROCKTON, ILLINOIS 61072
815/624-8431
389-2960

November 14, 1983

Ms. Dawn Dressler
571 Northwestern
So. Beloit, IL
61080

Dear Ms. Dressler,

In this season of miracles it is exciting to know that MIRACLES STILL HAPPEN!

I've seen them! CHILDREN who doctors said would NEVER WALK - not only WALKING, but RUNNING! Children who COULDN'T TALK - "TALKING" through sign language! Children who were described as "BEDRIDDEN", now able to MOVE THEIR OWN WHEELCHAIRS!

I've seen these MIRACLES right here with OUR OWN CHILDREN - YOUR FRIENDS.

YOU'VE been a part of these miracles because you've SUPPORTED OUR CHILDREN!

When JOHN came to us from a nursing home, not so long ago, he COULDN'T WALK. We were told he NEVER WOULD! He needed very special education and SPECIAL THERAPY. The local school could not provide it, so we did.

Today, John is not only WALKING - but RUNNING!! He's in OUR SCHOOL and doing VERY WELL - he has a BRIGHT FUTURE.

Another one of YOUR FRIENDS has a congenital heart defect. Doctors told Judy's mother she would NEVER LIVE to be a teenager. JUDY TURNED 20 THIS FALL!

Allen came to us from an unsuccessful placement in Oregon. He's an Illinois child, but when he went to Oregon no one in Illinois could or would care for him.

When Allen arrived he was scared, fought with staff and children and had no communication skills at all! We were told these problems would NEVER get better!

November 14, 1983

HUNDREDS of hours of hard work and several months later Allen STOPPED FIGHTING with staff and children. He obviously feels he is HOME. He has at least 25 WORDS and over 150 SIGNS. He doesn't just communicate - HE TALKS!!

These are just a few of the MIRACLES, and there are MANY OTHERS WAITING!

As 1983 draws to a close, you may be thinking of YOUR GIFT to our children. YOUR THOUGHTFULNESS this past year has provided many necessities for our children they would not otherwise have enjoyed.

Our young people, as all youth, have GREATER NEEDS as they grow older.

1984 will be a difficult year because of continued cutbacks in Social Service funding. We will continue to CUT EXPENSES whenever possible. Even with important cuts, we will be MORE DEPENDENT upon our friends like YOU.

I have enclosed a reply envelope that I hope you will find in your heart to use. The $10, $20, $30 or more you give today could make the difference of a MIRACLE for one of our children!

THANK YOU!

Sincerely,

John Holmstrom

John T. Holmstrom III, President
Board of Directors

JTH:ns

P.S. Please, use the envelope now! Your love can turn to a miracle!

GOLDIE B. FLOBERG CENTER FOR CHILDREN

December 5, 1983

Less than 3 weeks to Christmas and then the end of 1983!

I know you have a lot of requests tugging at you during the Holidays - not to mention all the things you have to do!

But if you could reconsider a gift to our children, I would be very grateful.

Your check in the enclosed reply envelope would brighten our Christmas.

Thank you for thinking of us, and may your future be as bright as ours.

GOLDIE B. FLOBERG CENTER FOR CHILDREN
58 WEST ROCKTON ROAD ROCKTON, ILLINOIS 61072
815/624-8431
389-2960

May 22, 1984

Ms. Dawn Dressler
571 Northwestern
South Beloit, IL
61080

Dear Ms. Dressler,

The Holiday season is always a delightful time of sharing. Your willingness to share with our young people is especially appreciated!

Your gift of $50.00 has not only brightened our Holiday, but has helped us to end the year successfully, and begin the new year with a bright promise!

The New Year is filled with opportunity for each one of our young people. Your thoughtfulness will encourage our youngsters to get the most from each challenge - because they know YOU care.

The enclosed gift is a token of appreciation from the children and me. We hope you enjoy it and think of our gratitude when you use it.

Thank you - and may your Holidays be as bright as our future.

Sincerely,

John T. Holmstrom III, President
Board of Directors

JTH:ns

encl.

An Outstanding 17% Response From Cold Prospects

Our best direct mail letter drew a 17% response total for groups mailed both with and without a supplementary brouchure. We were very pleased with this response, especially in view of the mailing date in late January.

Every fund raiser knows how important the holiday fund raising campaigns are to agency coffers. We had had a very successful direct mail campaign in November and December of 1983. However, due to our personnel resources, we try to send between 1,500 and 3,000 pieces per month on a regular basis—and this can pose a problem during the anti-climactic months after the holiday season.

In January, most people seem to be thinking about getting their bills squared away and preparing their income tax returns. But I hoped that they, like I, were sorry to see the holiday season depart and have everything return to "business as usual." I think this letter was successful because it gave recipients the opportunity to contine the momentum of fellowship that the holidays seem to spark. And, it also helped that we could use our Goodwill name as a starting point.

Finally, I should add that this mailing was not sent to our regular donor mailing list; the list we used was a "cold" list, which made our outstanding results even more gratifying.

Judi Bradac

GOODWILL INDUSTRIES
of Southern Los Angeles County
800 WEST PACIFIC COAST HIGHWAY • LONG BEACH, CA 90806-5299 • (213) 435-3411

January 25, 1984

Dear Friend,

Now that a new year has begun everyone is getting back down to business. The sparkling ornaments have been wrapped and stored, the gifts have been opened and put away, and we won't be hearing our friends and neighbors wishing us "Peace on Earth and Goodwill to all."

But Goodwill is not an ornament to be wrapped and stored on the back of a shelf out of sight. Goodwill is a gift that, when opened, will flourish every day all year long, and continue to grow with each passing year. Handicapped men and women who experienced the "miracle" of Goodwill years ago are still working today. Supporting themselves. Paying taxes instead of being supported by tax dollars.

At Goodwill Industries of Southern Los Angeles County, we know that rehabilitation isn't a miracle. It is an equitable and economically sound program for helping people become independent. As we begin our 55th year serving 36 cities -- including your community -- we need your help more than ever.

A disability could strike anyone: through industrial injury, heart attack, a car accident. Today, one out of every ten persons in this country has a disability. And, without your Goodwill, our ability to provide education, vocational training, evaluation, employment, counseling, job placement assistance, and daily living adjustment for handicapped men and women would be severely impaired.

Your gift today is a gift that will live on into the future by helping a disabled person become productive again. Or by helping a person who has been handicapped since birth become self-sufficient for the first time in his or her life...a true miracle of the human spirit.

Please don't hesitate. Many people have been waiting a lifetime for the opportunity to work and be a valuable part of our community. Goodwill is not just a season -- please live it with us all year long!

Sincerely,

Ruth C. Steinmetz

Ruth C. Steinmetz
President

Our business works. So people can.
A NON-PROFIT REHABILITATION FACILITY FOR THE HANDICAPPED
ACCREDITED BY THE COMMISSION ON ACCREDITATION OF REHABILITATION FACILITIES

Three-Fold Purpose Letter

This letter was used to accompany a brochure for our expansion/remodeling project at our sheltered and skilled care nursing facility. Though our mailing list had received information about the project on previous occasions, this personal letter was addressed to 1,000 top and/or consistent donors.

The purpose of the letter was three-fold:

One—To say thank you; to remind them of their past participation.

Two—To inform; to refresh their memories by summarizing components of the expansion/remodeling project.

Three—To encourage participation; to demonstrate that the welfare of the residents **and** the future of the organization were considered in the strategy for rasing money.

For the most part, direct mail appeal should be positive. People want to be a part of a success and like to know that their contribution, however small, is appreciated. A personal letter, signed by a visible member of the organization, can accomplish this.

Lynne M. Staley

St. Pauls House
3831 N. Mozart Street
Chicago, Illinois 60618
Tel. 478-4222

StPH/GCH

Grace Convalescent Home
2800 West Grace Street
Chicago, Illinois 60618
Tel. 478-0940

Jan. 30, 1984

Dear ________________, (Name of Top Donor)

It is a pleasure and a privilege to be writing to tell you about our proposed expansion and remodeling project scheduled to begin this year. It is the support of people like you that has laid the groundwork for St. Pauls House and Grace Convalescent Home to keep up with the growing needs and changes in nursing care. Thank you.

As you know, we will be adding a 51 bed nursing care wing and a combined dining room and kitchen; we will also be remodeling to expand our Occupational and Physical Therapy areas and to centralize our administrative offices. I hope the enclosed literature will present our plan in a little more detail.

We are proud of the fact that our residents' rates are some of the lowest in Chicago. We take pride in providing quality nursing care at reasonable rates. It is for this reason that our Board of Directors has decided to forego the high interest rates of commercial financing, use a portion of our endowment funds, and accept charitable contributions for the remainder of the project cost. With this in mind, I hope you will consider supporting us, again, as we plan for the future. Your support, as always, is greatly appreciated!

Sincerely,

Rev. Warren J. Mueller
Executive Director
WM/ls
Enclosure

First Venture Brings 2% Response And National Award

This was our first venture into direct mail fundraising: a trail balloon that surprised us with a two percent response and a national award from Goodwill Industries of America in 1983.

We had done no serious fundraising in recent years, because our services are financed primarily by the sale of donated goods. Most cash donations were voluntary, and intermittent.

The purpose of the "No Shoes" piece was to raise money for a scholarship fund, to solidify our prior donor base, and to develop a new donor constituency from subscribers to a high-status regional magazine.

I tried to follow all the rules: teaser on the envelope to get recipients to open it...a personal message...the postscript...individualizing by production on our word processor (possible because of the size of our mailing). It went to about 8,000 people in our limited three-county territority.

We did get that new constituency: 72 percent of the responses, and 62 percent of the dollars, came from new donors. Overall, gifts ranged from $5 to $500, with an overall average of $28. We did better than break even on the "prospecting" mailing; costs per dollar raised was 58 cents. And those new donors have been repeaters.

(Ms.) Lee Jones

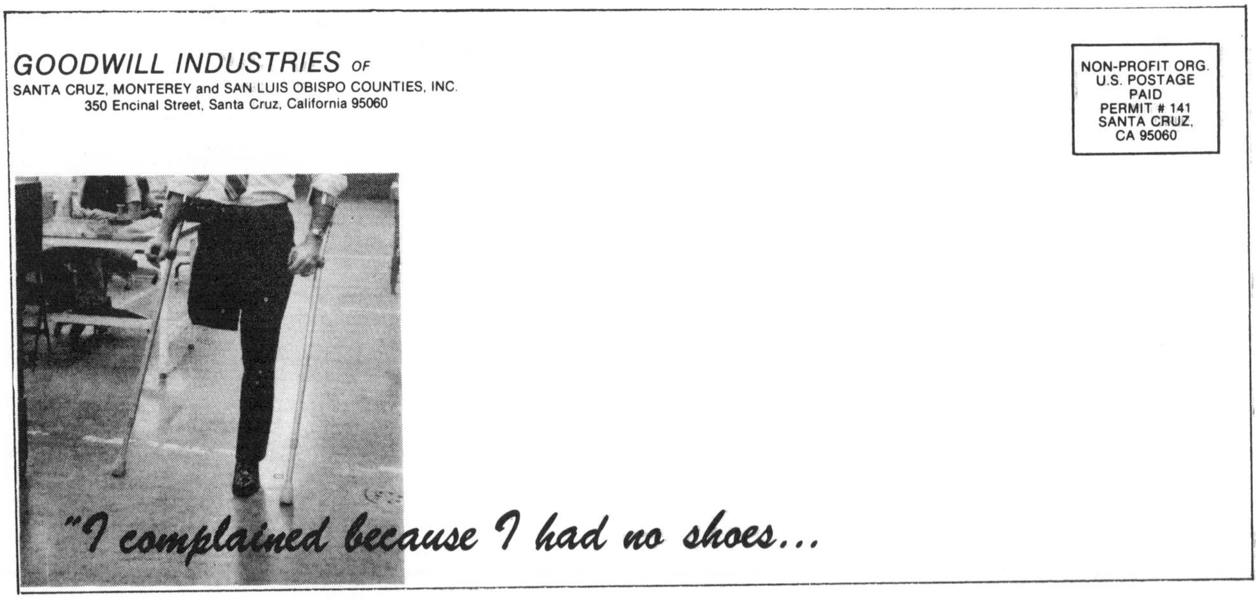
GOODWILL INDUSTRIES OF
SANTA CRUZ, MONTEREY and SAN LUIS OBISPO COUNTIES, INC.
350 Encinal Street, Santa Cruz, California 95060
NON-PROFIT ORG.
U.S. POSTAGE
PAID
PERMIT # 141
SANTA CRUZ,
CA 95060
"I complained because I had no shoes...

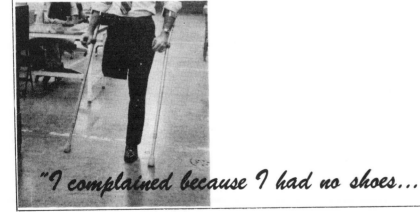

GOODWILL INDUSTRIES OF

SANTA CRUZ, MONTEREY and SAN LUIS OBISPO COUNTIES, INC.
350 Encinal Street, Santa Cruz, California 95060

goodwill

...until I met a man who had no feet."

Dear Mr. and Mrs. Bowers:

Perhaps your father taught you this when you were young. Mine did. It keeps things in perspective, and I have learned, in my better moments, not to complain.

But what of people who don't have feet they can walk on...or eyes that see...or backs that support their bodies? In my years of affiliation with Goodwill, I have discovered that disabled people don't complain, either. They are too busy, at important work. I am writing today to ask you to help them.

Goodwill's trainees are busy taking what life has handed them — whether through accident, illness or birth defect — and making the best of it. They're glad to have the chance to discover and develop all the good things about themselves, and to put these to productive use. This might mean running a switchboard from a wheelchair, doing intricate assembly with an artificial hand, or bookkeeping in a silent world.

A body may have limitations, but the power and potential of the human soul, when nurtured in an empowering environment, are limitless. Goodwill, with its rehabilitation programs, is that kind of environment for the handicapped of the Monterey Bay region.

Please help miracles to happen. Send the price of a pair of shoes — or two — or a dozen if you can — in the enclosed envelope to Goodwill's Rehabilitation Scholarship Fund. Your gift (whether $10 or $1,000) will put someone on the road to proud independence.

Remember, the handicapped don't complain. They ask only for the chance to help themselves. Your gift may not restore someone's feet, but when that person is earning a living despite their absence, it doesn't matter so much.

Thank you,

Colette Seiple
Chairman of the Board

P.S. In the next 30 days, we urgently need to hear from 1,000 people like you who are willing to give disabled people — not charity, but a chance to help themselves. Please help.

Holiday Mailing Brings Good Results

Hazard-Perry County Community Ministries, Inc., of Hazard, Kentucky, is a small Christian-oriented nonprofit organization that is dedicated to meeting human needs in our area. Funding for the programs and activities of H-PCCM come mostly through direct mail letters addressed to individuals, civic clubs, churches, and local businesses. Some city and county government funds are budgeted and a few government grants have been received for special emergency food programs. However, it is the DIRECT MAIL LETTER H-PCCM depends on for building a strong community base.

H-PCCM has found holidays to be an excellent time to direct a special fund letter for attracting new contributors. For example, H-PCCM recently adopted VALENTINE'S DAY as the holiday for contacting our local professionals. Enclosed is a copy of this year's appeal. The use of the attached heart-seal drew immediate attention to insure a reading, while the reference to the number of doctors, attorneys, and dentists, encouraged a friendly matching of professions for supporting our respected organization.

This year's letter attracted two new attorneys, four new doctors, one dentist, and increased contributions from those already on our support list as well as donations from some professionals who didn't give in 1983.

H-PCCM may be a small nonprofit organization, located in a small community, but we try to approach our fundraising in a professional manner.

Virginia Blankenship

HAZARD-PERRY COUNTY COMMUNITY MINISTRIES, INC.

P. O. Box 347

Hazard, Kentucky 41701

February 1984

Dr. James M. Jolly, Jr.
1724½ N Main Street
Hazard, Kentucky 41701

Dear Dr. Jolly:

It has been said: "When God measures man, He puts the tape around the ♥ instead of the head."

It is not surprising that Hazard-Perry County Community Ministries, Inc. chooses the month of February to contact its professional friends. DENTISTS, ATTORNEYS, DOCTORS. . . these are professionals who understand human needs.

H-PCCM is a local nonprofit organization dedicated to meeting human needs within the community. Be it the need for emergency food, blankets, quality child-care, outings for Nursing Home patients, grocery trips for Senior Citizens, youth recreation, and the construction of a YOUTH CENTER; H-PCCM is here to serve.

These needed services are available in our area because of the growing support of our community. In 1983, H-PCCM had the financial support of 4 lawyers and 2 doctors. In 1984, H-PCCM anticipates a measurable increase from the professional community.

Please consider the measure of YOUR HEART. Meeting human needs is a vital interest we share. A tax-deductible contribution of $25, $50, $100--can be a confident expression of a "giving" self. . . a bountiful heart.

Think about it. GENEROSITY is a measurable expression.

Yours truly,

Virginia Blankenship
Public Relations Secretary
Hazard-Perry County Community Ministries

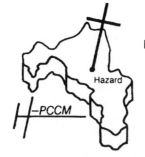

Annual Appeal Covers Special Financial Aid

This letter represents an annual campership appeal that is sent to area businesses and community friends.

The Pittsfield Girls Club offers four camps in the summer to all girls and boys regardless of race, creed, color or income. The Club offers financial aid and camperships to those with hardships. In order to assure that needy children are not turned away, an annual monetary appeal is necessary. Each year the Pittsfield Girls Club gives approximately $7,000 to $9,000 in camperships and financial aid.

The Department of Social Services, Department of Public Welfare, schools, churches, and many other agencies act as referral sources for needy families. The Club realizes almost enough money through contributions to match the amounts given out.

Susan R. Lampshire-Kates

PITTSFIELD GIRLS CLUB, INC.

"...To become someone you never expected but somebody else did."

May 12, 1984

Dear Ms. Jones:

This year, more than ever, outdoor camp experiences are important for girls.

The Girls Club is in a much better position. The enormous amount of work and love needed to start a new Bingo game for the benefit of the Club will eventually stabilize all program services. The Club has many debts, however, built up from years of struggling, your contribution is needed more than ever.

This is a crucial year. To keep the Camps in good operating condition, some rehabilitation must occur. Cabins, steps, boating beach, and roofs are some of the repairs needed to remain safe for the children.

Your camperships dollars are desperately needed so we are not forced to turn away girls. There are no spare monies to fund camperships from sources other than the community - businesses and individuals such as you.

Your contribution to send girls to Camps is tax deductible and will make a real difference.

Sincerely,

Edward W. Burniske, Jr., Chair
Camperships

Ann H. Trabulsi, President

mep

"Several years ago, one of my daughters was granted a partial campership to enable her to attend a two-week session. As she was one of six young children in our family we were finding it financially difficult at that particular time to send her to camp. She especially wanted to go as her best friend had enrolled.

At this time, I would also like to express my deepest appreciation to the Girls Club for the many fine benefits my four daughters derived from their attendance there while they were growing up..."

...Campership Contributor

BERKSHIRE
UNITED WAY, INC

165 East Street, Pittsfield, Mass. 01201 (413) 442-5174
Susan R. Lampshire-Kates, D.P.E., Executive Director

GIRLS CLUBS OF AMERICA

Informing Their Constituency

This letter is personalized because these people have a good giving history with York Place.

"Susan Palmer" is not the actual name but the letter is authentic with a few deletions to assure confidentiality.

It is important that our constituency know how successful we are in treating emotionally disturbed children and that they can feel an ownership in our ministry.

In a brief but effective way I was able to present a case record so that our constituency could better understand the type of children we work with.

York Place is a church owned institution which provides quality clinical services. Most of our supporters are Episcopalian so I put emphasis on our work as a shared ministry.

By suggesting specific sums for donation, we have greatly upgraded the $4 and $5 donations which used to cost us money to process.

This letter raised $10,000. More importantly, we received at least a dozen requests for additional copies of this letter from the women's groups in various churches to be used in raising money for York Place.

As a side benefit we received four letters of support and encouragement to be forwarded to the girl who wrote the letter.

The Rev. Craig C. Butler, ACSW, AAMFT

York Place — Episcopal Church Home for Children
A Residential Treatment Center
In the South Carolina Up-Country at York

H. Sanford Howie, Jr., ACSW
Executive Director

P. E. Knight
Director of Planned Giving

The Rev. Craig C. Butler, ACSW, AAMFT
Director of Family Enrichment and Development

Sherry A. Wicker, M.S.
Treatment Center Director

Brian L. Phelps, M.A.
Treatment Center Director

Michael J. Brockman, M. Ed.
Treatment Center Director

Christina H. Lowry, M.S.W.
Recreation and Intake Coordinator

Harry H. Wright, M. D.
Psychiatric Consultant

Patrick T. Butterfield, M. D.
Psychiatric Consultant

M. R. Newton, M. A.
Child Development Specialist

Ried Raben, Ph. D.
Family Therapy Consultant

March 1984

Dear Russell and Ofie:

Please read the following letter which I received recently from a young lady who was in placement at York Place nine years ago.

> *Dear Mr. Butler:*
>
> *I have some good news I would like to share with you, and that is, I, Susan Palmer, the person who everyone in the teaching field said wouldn't even finish high school, got a scholarship to college, and boy do I feel good about it! The other good news is that in March I should be in my own apartment.*
>
> *Well, Mr. Butler, I'm going to let you go now, I just thought it would be nice of me to drop you a line to let you know the progress I've made.*
>
> *Your friend,*
> *Susan Palmer*
>
> P.S. *I hope 1984 is going to be as great a year for you as I know it's going to be for me!*

When Susan entered the Episcopal Church Home, her presenting problems were epilepsy, asthmatic attacks, brain damage, dull/normal intelligence, a very depressed low self concept, self inflicted wounds, suicide gestures, extreme withdrawal, a stressful family life, and poor peer relationships.

How exciting it is to be a part of the miraculous process where God's healing power mends the broken spirits of young disturbed children and enables them to celebrate life again. Thanks to your support of York Place, 1984 will be a great year for Susan!

Won't you send a donation of $10, $25, $50, $100, or ___ today to York Place so that many more children with special needs will be able to have great years in the future.

Thank you for caring!

Yours in Christ,

Craig C. Butler

The Rev. Craig C. Butler, ACSW, AAMFT
Director of Family Enrichment and Development

CCB:dp

234 Kings Mountain Street
York, South Carolina 29745
(803) 684-4011

Letter Raises $163,700

This one-page letter was sent to 19,204 people from my mailing list who were $5 or more contributors. The response was 21.43% return (4115) for $128,700.19, making the average gift $31.28. I also received $35,000.00 as a matching grant (half the bill) from the Keiwit Foundation. **Total from this appeal—$163,700.00.**

My purpose was to take the reader through the letter as rapidly as I could to establish a sense of urgency about the specific crisis. I also wanted to acknowledge their past support and psychologically cement further relationship for future support. It was written in a personalized tone and with enough urgency to motivate fast response—most of the money came within 10 days.

Time was a major factor in getting this letter out. Both the carrier and the BRE were personalized, but I didn't have enough time to personalize the letter, which I ordinarily do. The letter was printed and sent first class.

While I don't feel this letter is the best thing I've ever done, I certainly can't argue with a 21.43% return, can I?

Bob Kilby

CHARTERED SEPTEMBER 1893

Building futures and providing homes and opportunities for Nebraska's children – statewide

Nebraska Children's Home Society

3549 FONTENELLE BOULEVARD · PHONE 451-0787 · OMAHA, NEBRASKA 68104

August 2, 1982

Dear Friend of Little Children,

This is a special letter to special folks like you who we consider to be very important friends of Nebraska Children's Home Society. I'm sure that you share an equal satisfaction in knowing that your support has helped to meet one of the greatest challenges in Nebraska - giving a new life to the many unfortunate children that look to us for help.

Usually, at this time of the year, we must ask assistance from our special friends to help with the bills until the Little Red Stocking Appeal is sent out near the end of the year. This year is no different - especially with the present economy such as it is.

But - this year we find ourselves facing an additional problem we weren't expecting.

After 59 years, the plumbing and furnaces at the Receiving Home gave up and must be replaced. Those who have visited the Home realized that while it has never been a "marble palace" it still served as a home to thousands of children through the years. We've always pinched every penny to make sure the children received the help needed instead of seeing how fancy we could make a four story building look. But, now we are past the cosmetic or band-aid treatment and must make the first major renovation since 1923.

Because of water damage inside the walls, we have to start the work immediately and the workmen tell us the cost will be approximately $70,000.

This is the reason this letter is coming to you a few weeks earlier than usual. We hope and pray that you will be able to help the Society with this badly needed renovation.

Hopefully,

John P. Ford
President

Donations For Food Program

I developed this letter to secure donations in support of an Emergency Food Pantry program. I believe it is effective for the following reasons:

1) It identifies an emotional problem and affords the reader an opportunity to directly impact that problem.

2) It provides documentation of the problem.

3) It is brief.

4) The entire point of the letter is contained in three (3) highlighted sections.

Within three months this mailing generated $4,956.00 in private contributions of cash and food for the program.

Rod Huenemann

upper des moines OPPORTUNITY inc.

A COMMUNITY ACTION AGENCY
Providing Opportunities For Self-Sufficiency

CENTRAL ADMINISTRATIVE OFFICE
905 Lake Street
P.O. Box 98
Emmetsburg, Iowa 50536
(712) 852-3866

BUENA VISTA COUNTY
504½ Lake Avenue
Storm Lake, Iowa 50588
(712) 732-1757

CLAY COUNTY
500 East Milwaukee
Spencer, Iowa 51301
(712) 262-7409

DICKINSON COUNTY
2000 Hill Avenue
Spirit Lake, Iowa 51360
(712) 336-4137

EMMET COUNTY
Courthouse, Box 32
Estherville, Iowa 51334
(712) 362-2391

O'BRIEN COUNTY
Courthouse, Box 117
Primghar, Iowa 51245
(712) 757-8845

OSCEOLA COUNTY
848 Third Avenue
Sibley, Iowa 51249
(712) 754-2573

PALO ALTO COUNTY
Tenth and Broadway
Emmetsburg, Iowa 50536
(712) 852-3482

POCAHONTAS COUNTY
25 Third Avenue N.W.
Pocahontas, Iowa 50574
(712) 335-4226

May 22, 1984

Dear Friends:

In March, the Iowa Department of Human Services released the results of the "Iowa Food and Hunger Survey". The survey was designed to gather information on the problem of hunger in Iowa and to develop appropriate recommendations concerning food aid.

The survey results confirmed many of our impressions of hunger in Iowa:

1) Hunger is a serious problem in Iowa resulting in health problems, family discord, and unpaid bills.
2) The #1 barrier to food is simply the inability to afford to buy food needed.
3) Most existing food programs are effective, but food amounts are not sufficient in some programs.

The survey results indicate **HUNGER EXISTS THROUGHOUT NORTHWEST IOWA.** In fact, 5 of the 8 counties in our area were included in the list of 38 Iowa counties having the **MOST EXTENSIVE HUNGER PROBLEM.**

You have been identified as someone who can make a significant contribution to the erradication of hunger in Northwest Iowa. We have initiated a campaign to secure additional regular donations of supplies for the Emergency Food Pantries in each of our County Outreach Centers. We would like to have your participation. **YOUR DONATIONS WOULD HELP FEED THE HUNGRY HERE IN NORTHWEST IOWA.** Additionally, any contributions of dated goods would help end waste in the food distribution chain. All donations are tax deductible.

We have enclosed further information about the operation of our Emergency Food Pantries and the results of the "Iowa Food and Hunger Survey" for your information.

Please give our request serious consideration and contact our County Office nearest you if you can help or if you have questions. Together we can help feed our hungry neighbors.

Warm Regards,

Kathleen T. Cackler

Kathleen T. Cackler
Executive Director

KTC:cc
Enclosure

Taking Advantage Of Attack

Our affiliate sends three direct mailings each year with an average return of $3,815. This piece raised $5,795, or 51% more than the average.

Following is our analysis of why this particular appeal was so effective:

Public opinion polls have, for the past several years, indicated that the great majority of Americans support a woman's constitutional right to obtain an abortion. In spite of this, a minority faction of anti-abortionists adopted increasingly belligerent methods of attacking supporters of reproductive rights. Among the tactics used locally were campaigns of harassment, such as erecting an anti-choice billboard in the same shopping center as our Planned Parenthood clinic.

Our initial reaction was to view this billboard as damaging to our clients as well as to our family planning program. Upon reflection, however, we realized that our many hundreds of supporters in this community would be as outraged as we were to the callous attack upon a woman's right to choose.

Consequently, we decided to capitalize on the lack of judgement shown by our opponents. We reproduced the offensive billboard and shared our indignation over its destructive message with our donors.

The results were more than gratifying.

Not only did contributions pour in, but letters of support and appreciation for our pro-choice position came as well. The letter raised half again as much as our average mail piece, and we are convinced that people give most generously when they become emotionally involved in an issue they care deeply about.

Sharon Ersch

planned parenthood of austin

Administrative Offices & Education Center
1309 East 12th Street, Austin, TX 78702 **(512) 472-0868**

Clinical Services
1823 East 7th Street, Austin, TX 78702 **(512) 477-5846**
1050 H South Lamar, Austin, TX 78704 **(512) 441-5421**

Dear Friend:

Attached is a picture of a billboard recently erected in the same shopping center as the new Planned Parenthood clinic in South Austin. It is outrageous that our clients, and the public at large, must be subjected to this kind of attack from anti-choice groups.

As the largest provider of family planning services in the city, Planned Parenthood of Austin is clearly the largest preventer of abortions as well.

But reason is lost on these anti-abortion fanatics. Their campaign of harassment has become better organized and more vicious. Across the nation, they have burned clinics, destroyed client records, picketed and harassed clients, and have been instrumental in reducing federal funding for family planning services.

We have been informed through our national organization that the anti-choice group PEACE (People Expressing a Concern for Everyone) announced that a nationwide wave of attacks against abortion clinics aimed at disrupting clinic operations would be launched September 17-18.

Disruptive tactics that were discussed included:

- Searching through waste discarded by clinics to obtain papers with patients' names in order to harass them.

- Carrying out a "blitz" in clinic waiting rooms by either subtly or overtly infiltrating clinic waiting rooms to counsel patients against abortion and distribute pamphlets and pictures of aborted fetuses to clinic patients.

Until recently, Austin has been spared from the brunt of these kinds of attacks. But no longer!

Our new clinic in South Austin has been besieged by picketers on a regular basis since its opening in mid-June. Picketers also maintained a several-hour vigil in front of the City Coliseum during our August fund raising event. We have been subjected to vile accusations in response to our recent membership mailings. And now these dangerous opponents of individual freedom have installed this offensive sign at our new clinic site. I'm sure you will agree that the sign is clearly designed to intimidate our clients and engender a climate of increasing intolerance in our city.

We must not ignore these insidious attacks upon individual freedom. The anti-choice fanatics are determined to pursue their goal of destroying individual reproductive freedom--at any cost--and force their "morality" on you and me. And, of course, those who will shoulder the heaviest portion of the burden are the poor and those Austinites who need our help the most.

You and I must act <u>now</u> to turn back the anti-choice groups' unrelenting assault. We must oppose them. If we remain passive, they will surely win.

That's why I'm writing this urgent letter to you today.

Planned Parenthood of Austin must raise $70,000 in the community this year. We must continue to provide family planning and education services to the thousands of low income men and women who need and want them and who have no other way to pay for their reproductive health care. We must help organize citizens to stand up <u>against</u> repressive legislation that would limit individual rights. We must conduct our <u>own</u> campaign, through the media and our public affairs network, in <u>support</u> of a woman's right to choose.

Your help is vital. Won't you send a contribution today.

Sincerely,

Beth Jenkins
Chair
1982 Fund Raising Committee

Christine Herlick Aubrey
President
Board of Directors

ANTI-CHOICE GROUPS STEP UP ATTACKS ON LOCAL PLANNED PARENTHOOD

Yes! I want to support Planned Parenthood of Austin in its fight to protect individual freedom.

Enclosed is my contribution.

- [ ] $60.64 provides birth control services to one woman for one year
- [ ] $169.75 provides an education session for 25 teenagers
- [ ] $27.25 allows Planned Parenthood of Austin to distribute a monthly public affairs alert to 150 people
- [ ] $250 will rent billboard space for one month
- [ ] $90 provides a physician for one birth control clinic
- [ ] Other $__________

Name____

Address____________________________________Zip__________

Raising Funds From Unions And Clubs

This letter was sent to union organizations and civic clubs as a fund raising effort for the Chemical People Project. I think it works primarily because it provides an easy way to give money. If an organization supports the goal "to reduce the loss of young lives, and potential, resulting from the abuse of alcohol and drugs," (and who wouldn't support such a goal?) all they need to do is pledge to buy a certain number of buttons.

They know what their money is buying and it is easy to document how the funds were expended. The letter also gives contact persons and a phone number should an organization need further information.

Tom Ansalt

THE CHEMICAL PEOPLE

Dear

The South Kitsap Chemical People Task Force is a group of parents, school representatives, professional and community leaders with concern about alcohol/drug abuse among youth. We are sponsoring drug abuse prevention programs, hoping that through education and by sponsoring drug free social activities we can reduce the loss of young lives, and potential, resulting from the abuse of alcohol and drugs.

We need your help to promote this important cause! We hope to raise funds for prevention activities through the sale of Chemical People buttons: "Hugs, Not Drugs." These buttons cost us 12-1/2 cents and we think we can sell them for 25 cents. For example, we hope to have a booth at the Air Fair next month to distribute resource information and hopefully sell buttons.

Will you help us get started through a donation so that we can buy our first supply of "Hugs, Not Drugs" buttons? At 12-1/2 cents each, $50 will buy 400 buttons, $125 will buy 1,000 buttons.

We hope to place our order within the next few weeks. If you would like a task force member present at your next meeting, we would be happy to arrange this. Simply call Julie or Diane at our message phone (479-3218) with your pledge or meeting time.

Thanks very much for any support you can give in combating this problem facing the youth of our community.

Sincerely,

South Kitsap Chemical People
Task Force

CO/ms

Tapping New Fund Raising Resources

I hope this letter will give an idea to others who are raising funds for a good cause. There are many worthy organizations and many untapped resources available to non-profit organizations. The more input on ideas of source tapping, the more finanacial aid will be received.

The return on this fund raiser was 43%. This is very high when compared to the national average of around 16%. The project was twofold. The auction put our center in the community spotlight. Slides of our programs and services were shown to people who attended. The hotels and motels received good publicity for their donations. The finanacial gain for the center was excellent.

Lonnie Oathout

Hope 7 Community Center
596 Pawling Avenue
Troy, New York 12180
~
Telephone (518) 272-8029

FIRST

DECEMBER

1983

Dear Sir:

Some of our members have had the pleasure of staying at your establishment and have frequently told us how much they enjoyed it.

Consequently, we are writing to inquire if you would help us in our work as a community center and, at the same time, publicize your fine establishment to the wealthiest members of our community.

We are holding our Annual Vacation Auction in March of 1984, and we are asking for the donation of a weekend vacation at any time convenient to you. In return for your vacation donation, we will display on one of our merchant's windows any brochures or pictures you may have. If you have a movie clip or slides available, we will be happy to show it the night of the auction to arouse further interest.

We know from experience that our Vacation Auction will be responsible for sending vacationers to many of the donating resorts. We know also, that aside from the satisfaction that comes from helping a community tackle its own problems, you will benefit by our telling your story to thousands of passersby and to over seven thousand who will receive our newsletter. May we hear from you soon?

Thanking you in advance for your kind consideration.

Sincerely,

Lonnie Oathout
Executive Director

LO/db

Hits A Responsive Emotional Chord

Here is the best copy I have written in the last few years.

The letter was highly successful. It generated just under $200,000 over a three month period from an active donor base of under 10,000.

I feel that the main reason the letter was so successful was that it hit a responsive emotional chord of the donors. The letter begins by stirring a memory that nearly everyone has and then merges that feeling into an emotional bond with the youth.

The letter gives what I feel are the basic requirements of a good appeal letter. They are:

1. Establishes an emotional bond between the donor and agency (youth).
2. States what the agency has been and is doing (services provided).
3. States the need and how the donor can help.

This and similar letters have been instrumental in increasing our donated income from $150,000 to nearly $500,000 per year in the last four years.

Darrell R. Hawkins

United Methodist

Youthville Inc.

Box 210 Newton, Kansas 67114

Robert H. Whitfield, Executive Director

Helping the Youth
of Kansas develop
Physically, Mentally,
Spiritually and Socially

Christmas 1981

Ms. Alice

Apt 2
KS 67124

Dear Ms.

Have you ever been so excited about something that you couldn't sleep? I'll bet when you were a child you spent many sleepless Christmas Eves in anticipation of the fun and gifts that were sure to be yours in the morning.

Many of the young people at Youthville will be sharing those feelings this Christmas for the first time. You see, for them, this will be the first Christmas they will feel "wanted" and "loved" by those around them.

For more than 50 years Youthville has been serving youth who have suffered the traumas of a broken home, physical and verbal abuse, rejection and constant failure. Many of these youth have given up HOPE!

At Youthville we take these youth with their low self-image and feelings of rejection. We build positive experiences for them. We give them lots of love, patience and understanding. In turn, they begin to have HOPE for a better future. What is HOPE?

<u>H</u> is for the happiness to know someone really cares.
<u>O</u> is for the opportunity to achieve attainable goals.
<u>P</u> is for the perseverance to overcome one's problems.
<u>E</u> is for the quality education available at Youthville.

You can give HOPE to these youth by sending a generous gift today! Due to drastic cutbacks in several of our funding sources, Youthville needs more than $350,000 to continue serving our present number of youth. Just $10 per day per student will help us provide HOPE for the future of these young people. How many days will <u>you</u> help provide?

As you prepare for the Christmas Season, please remember the boys and girls at Youthville again this year and consider the HOPE you can give them.

May the Peace and Joy of this Holiday Season be with you and your loved ones.

Sincerely,

Robert H. Whitfield

Robert H. Whitfield
Executive Director

RHW/dh

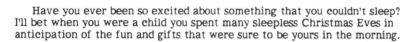

Works Well For Small Agencies

The enclosed Christmas gift solicitation letter works well as a format for agencies that are competing with larger agencies or businesses for support of worthwhile, but relatively small scale, programs. The following high points of the letter help to make it successful:

1) Note that the letter went out in July. This avoids the end of the year problem of losing donations because a merchant's donation "quota" has already been reached.

2) The letter contains general information about the program doing the soliciting.

3) The letter is short and quickly readable.

4) The letter gives background on previous donations. This acts as a motivating factor.

5) The letter emphasizes that donations are tax deductible and offers letters for use in the merchants' records.

6) A response date is given to prevent merchants from putting the request on "hold."

This letter has resulted in donations of toys, clothes, gifts, candy and checks totalling over $1,600, with more promised before Christmas. These donations, coupled with private donations, will enable over 1200 wrapped gifts to be distributed by the Women's Re-entry Program in December of 1984.

Cynthia J. Perrigo

July 16, 1984

Dear Friends,

MERRY CHRISTMAS!!!!!!!!!!

That's right! Here at the YWCA our 4th Annual Christmas Project is well underway. Throughout the year the Women's Re-entry Program, sponsored by the YW, provides job placement services, career training, referrals, workshops and counseling, without charge, to women throughout all of Lake County. Most of the women that we come in contact with are out on their own, trying to support themselves and their children. Because of numerous monetary strains, many of these women cannot afford to provide their children with a truely Merry Christmas. That's where we come in!

Last year, because of the generosity of local merchants and private citizens, the Women's Re-entry Program was able to provide over 800 brightly wrapped packages to our needy families. Of course, sorting, wrapping and delivering packages takes many, many hours. So-------this year we're starting extra early.

We are desperately in need of toys, clothing, wrapping paper, gift tags, candy, gift certificates, silk flowers and similar items. Any items that you could donate would be greatly appreciated. If you are unable to donate items, your cash donations will be put toward the filling in of any gaps that we may encounter. Of course, all of your donations are tax-deductible. We will be happy to furnish letters for your records regarding your donations, at your request.

We have set August 15th as a target date for having all donations in our office. If you could contact us by then, we would be happy to pick up your donation at your convenience.

We thank you for your help and support in the years past and hope that you will find it in your hearts to assist us once again. From the Women's Re-entry Program staff, program clients and all of their children, a hearty thank-you and MERRY CHRISTMAS!!!!!!!!!!

Cyndie — CYNTHIA J. PERRIGO, Director, Women's Re-entry Program

Tammy — TAMMY MORTENSEN, Employment Specialist, Women's Re-entry Program

HO! HO! HO! — SANTA

YWCA OF LAKE COUNTY
445 NORTH GENESEE STREET
(312) 662-4247
WAUKEGAN, ILLINOIS 60085
A United Way Agency
The Women's Center

Follows Basic Rules

In this membership letter we tried to follow some of the basic rules in direct-mail campaigns. The first sentence holds your attention—you learn the agency is successful and solutions to the problem already exist. Further, both clients and community leaders feel the service is valuable. The reader is urged to do something to support the agency **right now** and is asked to consider the impact of this problem on themselves and their neighbors.

This letter was sent to the entire mailing list (1,000). It brought in about 200 members. Most were either old members or persons who had personalized hand written notes from staff or Board urging them to join.

Mimi Hoffman

Rockland Family Shelter

for Victims of Domestic Violence
39 South Main Street, Spring Valley, N.Y. 10977 (914) 425-0112

Dear Friend,

If you believe victims of domestic violence in Rockland County should get the help they need, please read on.

Rockland Family Shelter has been working with victims of domestic violence for the past 2½ years. With our support, families formerly plagued with violence are now enjoying what many of us take for granted - peace and safety within their own homes.

We have found it is simply not true that domestic violence is one of those "impossible problems". Families we work with make important changes:

- 85% of the women we see at the Shelter don't require sheltering in the future.

- 80% of the women we've been able to reach through our follow-up study report no violence.

- And over 55% of the families we work with stay together.

One woman writes:

"The shelter was a turning point in my life. I was in crisis and they were the only ones who could help me. The shelter gave me all the information I needed to get help for myself, my husband and my children. It was one of the most helpful and moving experiences in my life - everyone pulling together to help one another."

And Family Court Judge, Alfred Weiner, now Supervising Family Court Judge of the 9th Judicial District, has this to say of Rockland Family Shelter:

"The Rockland Family Shelter has been in the forefront in the fight to assist battered women who but for this excellent

- continued -

United Way

organization would have no one to turn to. The work of the shelter has won the respect and admiration of the entire Rockland County community."

Rockland Family Shelter is committed to helping as many domestic violence victims as it can. So far Rockland Family Shelter has reached 500 families. We need your help so we can continue to reach more families.

Please fill out the enclosed application to begin or renew your membership in the Rockland Family Shelter community. Your membership dues will go directly toward keeping our shelter, hotline and Walk-In Center open.

Also, please tell your friends, family, neighbors and colleagues about what services we offer. They might need our help...research shows approximately one in six Rockland families (an alarming 46,000 people) could use the services we offer. They are:

*Hotline

*Shelter

*Walk-In Center

*Children's Services

*Speakers Bureau

*Groups

*Support Services (Task Oriented Counseling, accompaniment to court and other agencies)

*Training to Service Providers

Thank you for supporting our work and helping us to reach those in our community who no longer have to organize their lives around avoiding physical injury.

Sincerely,

Carolyn Fish
Executive Director

Steve Abel
President

CF/SA/jr

Two Successful Letters

The "Pool Steps" letter was mailed to the 500 names on our special contribution list. Responses came fast and furious—from $2.00 to $100, and we had our pool steps paid for in record time. Newspapers picked up on the story and the YWCA also received good free publicity. We believe the letter drew so well because of the opening couplet. We were also told that three original signatures on the letter helped greatly.

On the second letter, it was the joke that did it. Letters went out and money came in. And isn't that what it's all about.

Daisy A. Horn

YOUNG WOMEN'S CHRISTIAN ASSOCIATION

232 EAST FRONT STREET • PLAINFIELD, NEW JERSEY 07060 • (201) 756-3836

Summer, 1982

Dear Friend:

"Please Stop! Read this! Don't throw it away!
We need you to help others today.
Our cause is a good one, our resources few
For many depend on friends like you."

The YWCA swimming pool, built in 1925, is being used monthly by hundreds of people. Using the toe-holds in the pool wall, lively youngsters and agile oldsters climb in and out of the water with ease. But what about ----------

Persons with Arthritis who participate in water exercises through the YWCA's ALIVE Program?

Children with disabilities who learn to swim in the YWCA pool?

Parents with infants who attend the YWCA Baby Swim?

Adults lacking good muscle coordination and strength who want to swim in the YWCA pool?

Seniors who wish to exercise by swimming?

In hopes of assisting persons who would like to use our pool, but find getting in and out awkward or IMPOSSIBLE, we want to install portable steps with hand rails.

Will you help us raise $2,200 for this project?

Sincerely,

Elizabeth McNish
YWCA Board President

Daisy A. Horn
Executive Director

Lois Fischer
Director of Swimming & Physical Education

Yes, I want to help others not as fortunate as myself to swim in the YWCA pool.

Enclosed is my donation of $ __________.

Name ______________________________ Phone # ______________

Address ______________________________

"Here's another of our important Facts
This gift can be deducted from your Income Tax!"

MEMBER OF UNITED COMMUNITY FUNDS

YOUNG WOMEN'S CHRISTIAN ASSOCIATION

232 EAST FRONT STREET • PLAINFIELD, NEW JERSEY 07060 • (201) 756-3836

Dear Friend of the YWCA:

Shortly after the latest price increase on heating oil, a fuel company received an inquiry from the Mother Superior of a Convent:

"How much," she asked, "has the price of oil gone up?"

Wanting to break the news gently, the salesperson asked, "Are you sitting down, Sister?"

Replied the nun, "I'm kneeling".

In its struggle to become energy efficient and cost conscious, the YWCA has initiated priorities to be achieved as funds become available.

This Spring we intend to convert the pool heating system from the oil burner to a separate gas heater. This will enable us to eliminate using great quantities of oil to fire the burner to generate enough steam and also to completely shut down the unit during the warmer months.

Would you help us raise the $3,100 necessary? We have enclosed a pre-paid envelope for your donation and remind you that all gifts are tax deductible.

Sincerely,

Daisy A. Horn
Executive Director

DAH/rac

Enclosed please find $____________ to be included in the Pool Heater

Conversion Fund.
Name ____________________ Address ____________________

MEMBER OF UNITED COMMUNITY FUNDS

After Four Year Lapse. . .Success

Hopefully, the letter will not be the "BEST" that Inner City Ministry will ever do, but my staff urged me to enter it in your competition as the **first** letter sent by me since assuming the position of Executive Director some fifteen months ago. There had been no direct mail fund raising project, or any other fund raising event, from Inner City in over four years, so you can imagine our "qualms" when this letter was mailed.

It was sent to 1523 people and our percentage of return was 9%. We felt it was a good letter because it told a true story, and the subject matter and the season of the year were perfectly matched.

To say the least, we were in a state of "Happy Shock" with the fianacial response to our efforts. It has given us the enthusiasm, and heart, to go forward with more much needed plans for fund raising for this worthwhile organization.

Melody McDermitt

inner city ministry waco

P.O. BOX 85 – 817-752-0316 – WACO, TEXAS 76703

BREAK HERE

salt
CONTAINS: SALT, SODIUM SILICO ALUMINATE, TRI-CALCIUM PHOSPHATE.

Ye are the salt of the earth...

Matthew 5:13

MELODY McDERMITT
EXECUTIVE DIRECTOR

November 11, 1983

Dear Friend:

Just as salt makes a difference in the taste of food, so can you make a difference in the life and health of a homebound senior citizen.

"Not all of God's angels are in heaven," said Mrs. Williams, "some cook and deliver meals three times a week." Mrs. Williams is 77. She recently lost her leg due to cancer. She gets around in a wheel chair. Mr. Williams is 81 and has had several strokes. He uses a walker. He is hard of hearing. Mrs. Williams remains an optimistic person although, with both of them having difficulty, it's been really tough. Receiving meals on wheels helps in meeting their nutritional needs. After a recent hospital stay, Mr. Williams is gaining much needed weight. They give the credit to Inner City Ministry's Meals-on-Wheels program. Meals-on-Wheels brings contact with the outside world. It lets them know someone cares.

The story is true - the names have been changed. The Williams are only one example. There are 400 "stories." Inner City Ministry's Meals-on-Wheels program serves 400 meals each Monday, Wednesday and Friday. That's 62,000 meals in a year. Many who receive meals are alone and unable to prepare a hot, nutritious meal. They are lonely and have felt forgotten.

During this time of Thanksgiving as you think about your family and friends gathering together around a food-laden table, remember the old who are alone and unable to prepare meals; remember the sick; remember the hungry. You can make a difference. You can help bring a meal and caring concern through your contribution. A contribution of $10. provides the food for the meals three times a week for one month. A contribution of $120. would help us provide a meal three times a week for a year. It is our prayer that those who have supported Meals-on-Wheels in the past will not become tired of the continuing need for support and that this letter might reach many new friends interested in helping others.

Won't you be an angel and help us help others?

Sincerely,

Melody McDermitt
Executive Director

MMC:dm

P.S. Please place your check, that will provide meals, in the enclosed envelope and mail it. It does not require a stamp. Thank you for your concern.

Hospitals and Health Related Organizations

Seeds Make The Difference

The annual Spring Mayflower appeal of Swedish Medical Center Foundation is a familiar sight to long-time supporters of Swedish.

In the rapidly expanding south metropolitan Denver service area, we decided to cultivate new friends for the medical center through the 1984 Mayflower campaign. This was accomplished with an informative appeal designed to stimulate the responses of south metropolitan residents unacquainted with Swedish.

The appeal letter was designed to provide background information on Swedish Medical Center, with an explanation of the Mayflower tradition within Swedish. Letters were sent to 10,000 new households targeted by zip code, in addition to 23,000 current donors.

Packets containing seeds of the Colorado state flower were included with half of the mailing and half did not include seeds. Letters were composed with two different closing paragraphs, reflecting that variation.

The 1984 Swedish Mayflower appeal has been successful from several standpoints. A total of 28 new donors responded to the appeal. The average gift increased $.72 over 1983 contributions.

It was determined that letters containing seed packets were highly effective, as demonstrated in a 15% higher rate of response and average gift of $1.15 greater than responses to letters without seeds.

Most significant were the renewed gifts of 43 previous donors who had not made a contribution to the Foundation in two to three years.

The 1984 Swedish Medical Center Foundation Mayflower appeal served to cultivate new friends, renew the support of old friends and to increase the general level of financial support to the Foundation.

We will continue this format for the 1985 appeal and next time everyone will receive seed packets!

Victoria L. Turnipseed

Editor's Note: This entry was awarded Third Prize.

Hope Springs Eternal. Your Friendship Brings Hope.

May 10, 1984

Dear Friend:

When most of us think of the Mayflower, images of pilgrims and Plymouth Rock come to mind. But at Swedish Medical Center, the spirit of the Mayflower symbolizes a very special springtime tradition.

In its early roots as Swedish Consumptive Sanatorium, the hospital provided care to hundreds of persons suffering from tuberculosis. These individuals who came to sunny Colorado "chasing the cure" believed in the hope of healing that the Sanatorium offered.

In the Spring of 1922, Bede Hallberg, a charitable Swedish woman sympathetic to the many needs of tubercular patients, introduced the tradition of "Majblomman" to Swedish Consumptive Sanatorium. "Majblomann," the Swedish word for Mayflower, promoted the sale of hundreds of tiny celluloid flowers of Swedish origin to benefit Sanatorium patients.

The appeal of the Mayflower grew and the annual Spring sale of Swedish flowers supported the construction of the Mayflower Pavilion in 1930, which still graces the campus of Swedish Medical Center.

Today, Swedish Medical Center continues to provide hope and caring to thousands of patients from throughout the Rocky Mountain region. Tuberculosis has become a disease of the past, and now we help bring over 3,000 new lives into the world each year. We provide critical monitoring of premature infants in our neonatal intensive care nursery. We offer mental stimulation and emotional support to older individuals suffering from Alzheimer's disease. And we provide lifesaving resuscitation to the victims of accidents and neurotrauma.

To fulfill our mission to provide the finest, most progressive medical services available to you and your loved ones, we need your help. We ask your support to keep the spirit of the Mayflower alive this Spring, so that others less fortunate may grow strong and healthy again.

Your tax deductible contribution of $25, $50, $100 or more will greatly assist us. Just complete the enclosed reply card and return with your check in the envelope provided for your convenience.

I am enclosing a small packet of seeds for your Spring garden. Much like the tiny celluloid flowers of "Majblomman" that have grown throughout the years to make Swedish Medical Center highly respected in the field of health care, these seeds symbolize the hope and renewal that your gift will cultivate. It is our way of saying thank you for sharing in the hopeful spirit of the Mayflower. And thank you for your friendship.

Best of health,

Harris Cohn
Chairman
Swedish Medical Center Foundation
Board of Trustees

Swedish Medical Center Foundation

For additional information, please call 789-6666.

A Most Difficult Subject

Here is a small but effective direct mail piece.

The Christopher Letter represents an attempt to deal with a difficult subject, that of childhood death, in a positive, sensitive and honest format. We chose a monarch size personal letter with blue ink to neutralize the effect of the picture. The letter told a true story, was short, to the point, and made a direct appeal for funds.

We mailed five thousand units and received just short of $7,000 from the appeal.

Dick Perrier

San Diego Hospice
3243 Mission Village Dr.
San Diego, California 92123

(619) 560-0302

Christopher died recently and his twenty-three year old mother grieves at the loss of her eleven-month old baby. But she hasn't been alone — Hospice was there with her throughout, helping care for Christopher, supporting the family and working to ease the pain. Hospice continues to provide counseling and bereavement support and will be there until the pain of that loss can be accepted.

You were there, if you were a Hospice supporter; you made it possible for help to be there for Christopher and his family.

No one expects a child to die, so when it happens, it is rare there is any financial payment for the care, but Hospice is there anyway. You can make it possible for us to be there for the next child, the next family, the next parent.

Christopher is symbolic of all the other patients and their families your dollar amount supports this year. Your continued help may be the most important human, loving gift you can make.

Doris Howell, M.D.
President of the Board
San Diego Hospice Corporation

Wins Gift In Kind

Here is my "best" direct mail letter. Why is it the best?

1. **It's concise.** The one page shows this busy man that we appreciate his time.

2. **It's well researched.** It has the correct spelling of his name and proper title of his committee. It tells him we know of his cash gift to our Atlanta office.

3. **It flatters.** In the first paragraph it tells him his products are the best. He works hard to sell those products. It thanks him for his hard work.

4. **It tells him we are conscientious.** We are a non-profit organization, yet we are at **his** machines 12 hours a day. He can relate to other hard workers.

5. **It makes a direct appeal.** In the third paragraph it tells him we don't have the money to buy his product. In the fourth paragrph it tells him specifically what we want.

6. **It describes abstract benefits of his gift.** His company is getting something of value. It implies that his gift will allow us to raise more money to fund research which may some day save his own life.

7. **It allows him to choose a concrete benefit.** Does he want a plaque, newsletter article, or just a "thank you" note? It's his option.

The results were that his gift in kind is being installed next week!

Samuel V. Tannenbaum

5220 Biscayne Boulevard Miami, Florida 33137 (305) 751-1041

American Heart Association
Of Greater Miami, Inc.

March 26, 1984

Ms. Sylvia Shaw
Public Service Materials
111 North Central Avenue
Hartsdale, N.Y. 10530

Dear Ms. Shaw:

Lanier Business Products has provided the Heart Association with two No Problem Word Processors that have become the super stars of our office equipment.

Our staff is so enamoured with "their" Laniers that we have had to allocate specific time slots for operating the machines from 7:00 A.M. to 7:00 P.M.

We do not have the resources available to purchase another Lanier, and we are prohibited from directly soliciting your company because of your generous gifts to the Atlanta Heart Association.

We would appreciate your consideration of a gift in kind. Specifically, we are requesting a Super Smart Disc and a corresponding Memory Board.

Such a gift would allow us to upgrade our system, which, in turn, would lower our administrative costs, so more of our funds could be channelled into our primary focus of cardiovascular Research, Education and Community Service Programs.

Lanier would be recognized for this significant gift in manner deemed most appropriate by yourself and the Donations Committee.

We await your favorable response.

Sincerely,

Samuel V. Tannenbaum

Samuel V. Tannenbaum
Development Director

WE'RE FIGHTING FOR
YOUR LIFE

$25,000 From 250 Contributors

This letter resulted in contributions totalling $25,000 from approximately 250 contributors. Some gifts were solicited in person following receipt of the mailing. It was sent to 1,000 residents known to be Clinic supporters and community leaders. This represented the agency's first venture in direct mail.

Gary M. Bess

CO-CHAIRMEN:
Mayor ProTem Russ Lesser
William Christopher
(Father Mulcahey, MASH)

Armando Acosta
Councilman George Barks
Jack Belasco
Senator Robert Beverly
Laurie Bitter
David Britton
Wally Brown
Councilman Gary Brutch
Maria Calvano
Councilman Ronald Cawdrey
Marguerite V. Charnley
Bart Christensen
Kevin Cody
Rafael L. Cortada, Ph.D.
Mayor ProTem James Cragin
Elizabeth Davidson
Councilman Donald L. Dear
Jack Dirksen
Cindy DeNuno
Mayor Barbara Doerr
The Reverend Jack A. Eales
Richard Frank
Justine Frankel
Richard Fruin
Michael Gold, Ph.D.
James T. Goss
Donald Green
Alexander Haagen
Richard E. Hamilton, Jr., M.D.
Tom Heiser
Mayor C.R. "Bob" Holmes
David Asper Johnson
Ian Kramer, M.D.
John Lacy
Donald Landolfi
Dee Lococo
Mike Lococo
Jean McMillan
James Miller
Richard Neal, M.D.
Steve Nordeck
Noel Palm
Gene Parks, M.D.
Myron Pullen
Nan Rieman
Barbara Sayad
Mayor George Schmeltzer
Carol Schoenfeld
Larry Schoenfeld
Donna Schoonover
Clayton Shepherd
Richard Sivas
Councilman Archie Snow
Ron Sommer, M.D.
Lois Swanson
Councilman Mike Sweeney
Councilman William Switzer
Jan Teagardin
Mary Tyson
Councilman James Walker
Lance Widman
Richard W. Zalar, Jr., M.D.
Adrienne Ziegler

south bay free clinic patrons program

Dear Friend:

The SOUTH BAY FREE CLINIC needs your help.

This appeal is prompted by cutbacks in government funding which treaten the CLINIC's ability to maintain its program of health and human services to our community's needy. (See newspaper article enclosed). We are at a critical juncture. For 14 years the CLINIC has quietly, confidentially served more than 250,000 persons from all walks of life: teenagers in transition to adulthood; the elderly unable to afford timely health care; young mothers in need of prenatal services; the newly unemployed without health insurance for themselves and their families; and thousands of others who depend on the CLINIC to be there.... to care.... to listen.... and to help.

We hope that you too will be there. Please care, please listen, and please help.

This is your invitation to join the CLINIC's patrons program. A contribution of $25 or more will entitle you to attend a special holiday reception as our guest at the Manhattan Beach Country Club on Sunday, December 4, 1983, from 1 to 6 p.m. More importantly, however, your gift will support this vital community service which is an integral part of the south bay's network of community agencies.

Enclosed for your convenience please find a self-addressed postage paid envelope. If your gift cannot be made immediately, a pledge at this time will give us assurance that the CLINIC will be able to continue, as it has, at the forefront of cost-effective professional services.

Sincerely,

Mayor Pro Tem Russ Lesser
Manhattan Beach

William Christopher
(Father Mulcahy, "MASH")

1807 MANHATTAN BEACH BOULEVARD • MANHATTAN BEACH, CALIFORNIA 90266 • (213) 318-2521

Recovering Old Friends

This summer we computerized our donor list, and in the process ended up with 650 names of people who had donated to us in the distant past, but who had not donated in the past three years, and were not on our current donor list.

I decided to send out an inexpensive mailing to them with "address correction request" indicated, hoping to pick up a few good names to add to our current donor list. We did the printing ourselves on a mimeograph, and sent it out bulk mail at a total cost of $61.75. We received a total of $1,021 from 33 responses so far, an average donation of $30.91, and return rate of 5%. We are pleased to pick up a few old friends and a little extra money for such a small investment and so little effort on our part.

Phyllis J. Robb

National Multiple Sclerosis Society
Northern Indiana Chapter

Phyllis J. Robb, Executive Director
3554 Wells Street • Fort Wayne, IN 46808 • (219) 482-3757

August 1984

Dear Friend,

"Alice," a local 68 year old widow with MS, is severely handicapped and has regressed steadily since her diagnosis in 1936 to the point where she now needs daily nursing care. In addition to being confined to a wheelchair, she is legally blind. Her income is limited to $326 per month.

Her greatest pride is her home, a pre-civil war structure of great historical significance. It is very important to Alice to avoid nursing care as long as possible and to stay in the surroundings which are so dear to her.

Alice does have one hope for a secure future - people like you whose hearts are moved by her plight, and who reach out to help her through regular membership in the National Multiple Sclerosis Society.

With your previous gifts to the National Multiple Sclerosis Society we have been able to help Alice by arranging for an assistant to stop by each morning to help her with her daily routine. At the same time your dollars help to fund research into the cause and cure of this mysterious crippler, and fund local community programs that improve the quality of life for the more than 1,000 persons like Alice who suffer from Multiple Sclerosis in northern Indiana.

All many persons with Multiple Sclerosis need is a helping hand along the way, and that's what you can give them. Through the work of the National Multiple Sclerosis Society persons with Multiple Sclerosis are helped to cope with the effects of their disease and live life as fully as possible.

Please use the enclosed donor envelope to send your membership renewal today. We shall put it to good use, I assure you. Thank you for your help.

Sincerely,

Phyllis Robb

Phyllis J. Robb
Executive Director

Serving MS persons in the following counties: Adams, Allen, Benton, Carroll, Cass, DeKalb, Elkhart, Fulton, Huntington, Jasper, Kosciusko, LaGrange, Lake, LaPorte, Marshall, Miami, Newton, Noble, Porter, Pulaski, St. Joseph, Starke, Steuben, Wabash, Wells, White, Whitley.

Focussed On Hospital's Specialities

A mere two months of employment at Lubbock General Hospital and I was assigned a direct mail piece.

Since hospitals are so specialized, it is terribly difficult to do something different in this line; so my supervisor and I collaborated. We decided that the easiest way to do something different is to present real life situations, because every individual case is just a little bit different. Aside from that, case studies add a personal touch, bringing the reader closer to the person in the study.

We decided to focus on two of our specialities offered at only Lubbock General Hospital in the city of Lubbock—our Emercency Medical Services and our neonatal intensive care unit.

We then arrived at the very lowest dollar amount to allow membership into the Lubbock General Hospital Foundation, and would still be cost effective, but we sent it at year's end (tax deduction time) as an incentive to send more.

Not only did the Christmas letter raise needed funds, but brought attention to our special services. The prestigious signature of a town leader and our new Foundation Chairman introduced him to our public.

Jill Hinckley

Lubbock General Hospital
FOUNDATION
P.O. Box 5980 Lubbock, Texas (806) 743-3322

December 15, 1983

Dear Friend:

James Benford is 66. Angela Williams is only a few months old.

Although generations apart, these two have something in common—both will be celebrating Christmas at home with their families.

Four years ago, Mr. Benford began experiencing chest pains and having difficulty in breathing so he called the Emergency Medical Services at Lubbock General Hospital. Upon arrival at Lubbock General, Mr. Benford went into cardiac arrest. The combined efforts of E.M.S. Paramedics and the Emergency Room staff restored Mr. Benford's heartbeat.

After a succession of heart problems, Mr. Benford had open heart surgery. Today he says he is in great health.

Almost three months premature when she made her grand entrance in the world on August 31, 1983, Angela's chances were slim. In the delivery room, a special neonatal intensive care staff was on hand with life-support equipment. A tube was inserted in Angela's airway to assist in breathing and she was immediately put on a respirator. At 2-weeks-old, tiny Angela required heart surgery. At one point her weight dropped to 1 pound, 10 ounces.

But Angela was not through with this world yet. In 45 days she was off the respirator and by November 19, the Williams had their little angel home.

In emergencies, the efficiency with which the skilled medical personnel handle the situation is only made possible with the proper equipment.

A gift of $25.00 or more will entitle you to become a member of the Lubbock General Hospital Foundation, a non-profit organization established to help the hospital help others by purchasing life-saving equipment.

So this Christmas, give the gift of life—give to the Lubbock General Hospital Foundation.

The Benfords and the Williams extend their most heartfelt thanks.

Sincerely,

W.B. "Dub" Rushing
Foundation Chairman

P.S. Your gift to the Lubbock General Hospital Foundation is tax deductible.

Giving Special Recognition

Friends of the Family is a special, small membership group as the letter explains. A strength of this letter is that it makes it clear that the person being solicited would be part of a special group who are recognized in special ways, even if they are not spectacular. The letter also manages to sneak in a couple of appeals that we frequently use in approaching other individuals and almost always use when going to corporations and foundations.

The letter mentions our Family and Child Clinic and our largest program that attracts donations, free care of the indigent. We don't push it, but it's there nonetheless. Also there is mention of our status in relation to Northwestern Memorial Hospital. We have problems raising funds often because those we approach think that we are part of a huge hospital that basically approaches everyone for money—and usually gets it. We point out that this is not the case. This appeal is simple and clear and often cuts through all the discussion, which ultimately is very complicted, concerning our relationship to the Hospital.

Finally, the letter comes from a Board member who is also a member of the Friends. Enclosed information also says more about all facets of our programs and needs.

This particular letter did **not** succeed. This person did not choose to join the Friends. But of the letters similar to this that we sent out—and we vary their contents a little, depending on the person and the time of year—our response rate was 50% or more. For us that is good, because this is a supplemental mailing to our annual solicitation.

John Jacob

Suite 1530, 666 North Lake Shore Drive, Chicago, Illinois 60611 (312) 649-7285

July 3, 1984

Mr. Noboru Honda
3525 W. Peterson Avenue
Chicago, Illinois 60659

Dear Mr. Honda:

I hope that you will consider joining our membership group the Friends of The Family Institute of Chicago. It consists of those individual donors interested in mental health training, therapy, and research who contribute $100 or more during a given calendar year. Our Friends group is small but very important. Funds raised from the Friends are used to offset deficits incurred by our Clinic, which has been treating a large number of indigent patients for no fee.

All Friends receive membership designations and all announcements of workshops, new training programs and seminars, and our Board newsletter. Friends also are entitled to discounts on our workshops and other presentations. Finally, the Friends meet once a year at a special event--usually something that is more social than professional. We have a broad range of supporters who share in common their philanthropy in this field.

The Center for Family Studies is a cost center of Northwestern Memorial Hospital; as such, it receives no subsidies and is responsible for generating its own revenue. As a result, we often lose money and find it hard to find contributors because many assume that we are financially supported by the Hospital. Such is not the case.

Please let me know if you have any questions about us or about the Friends. I have enclosed some information that I hope you find enlightening. I hope to hear from you soon.

Sincerely,

Carolyn L. Wollaston

Carolyn L. Wollaston, Chair
Friends of the Family

CLW/jj
Enclosures

Member of the Northwestern Memorial Group
Member of the McGaw Medical Center of Northwestern University

Center for Family Studies/ The Family Institute of Chicago

Institute of Psychiatry
Northwestern Memorial Hospital

Tax Saving Helps. . .

But Not Real Reason For Success Of This Letter

I don't know if this is "the best" fund raising letter I've ever written, but it is one that I was very satisfied with, not only in its composition, but also in its results.

As you might guess from its date—Dec. 15—it was a late letter. Actually, it was a last minute sort of letter, written under pressure to get it out. I'd just resumed serving this client and the client wanted to get some solicitation into the mail before year-end. This was the result.

The letter was sent first-class to 385 past donors on our list who had not made a contribution in the current year (1983). Eighty, or just over 20 percent, replied with a contribution. The total contributed was $1,440, for an average gift of $18. Not bad at all!

Cost of production was low. We ran the letters off on Hospital letterhead using the office photocopier, then individually addressed each one on the office typewriter. Outside envelopes also were individually addressed by typewriter—admittedly slow, but the list wasn't long and the typing didn't take long. We had it out in less than a day, once copy was approved. A postage-paid, pre-addressed return envelope was enclosed. Cost of materials and production (not counting personnel time, which would have been paid whether we did the letter or not) was $173.25.

Despite the success of the letter, I'm not a fan of end-of-year-tax-savings letters. I don't really believe people make charitable contributions with the tax deduction in mind. I really believe people would continue to give to charitable causes even if the income tax deduction was repealed. I think the success of the letter comes from the second paragraph that reports on the success-to-date of our Expansion Fund and the appeal to finish it and meet our goal. And I repeat that appeal in paragraphs three and four. The tax savings promise in the letter, I think, serves as a spur to the recipient to "act now," before the end of the year, which was just days away.

Contributions continued to be received throughout the following month of January, lending support to my contention that the tax-savings aspect was not that important to these donors.

Donald F. Flathman

December 15, 1983

WEST
PARK
HOSPITAL
Ford Road and Fairmount Park, Philadelphia, Pa. 19131 (215) 878-0501

A CONTRIBUTION THIS YEAR WILL SAVE YOU MORE IN TAXES,
AND MAKE YOU FEEL GOOD.

It's true. A tax-deductible contribution in 1983 will save you more in income taxes than a contribution made next year. Why? Simple. The federal income tax rate is scheduled to go down next year. That means your taxes won't be higher; they'll be lower, on the same amount of income. And that's good news. But there's more! Because the tax rate is higher this year, every deduction you can take is worth more to you because it reduces a higher tax. So,

to save money,
take as many deductions as you can this year ...

including charitable deductions, like the contribution you made earlier to our Expansion Fund. Your contribution helped boost us toward our goal of raising $1-million for our new building, and we're grateful for your help. With it we've raised more than $700,000! That's quite an achievement ... enough to get things started. But the building's not finished, and neither is our fund raising. But we're still building. And we're still asking for contributions. We won't be satisfied until our $1-million goal is met. They're both getting close but ... we're not done yet!

A contribution made this year -- before Dec. 31 -- will save you money you'd otherwise have to pay to the government in taxes ... and it will move us closer to our goal of providing our community with an enlarged and modernized hospital with expanded health care services -- a goal I know you share.

That gives you two good reasons to do it again. And here's another: It feels good! To get that good feeling ... and a tax deduction too ... help your hospital reach its goal ...

Match your last contribution to West Park with another.

(Please turn page)

Affiliated with the Medical College of Pennsylvania

Page 2

Or enlarge on it a bit and get an even better feeling. On April 15, Income Tax Day, you'll be glad you did. But to get it you have to act fast and do it before Dec. 31. If you put it off you'll miss this chance. But if you do it today, you'll feel good all year long.

Have a happy and prosperous new year.

Sincerely,

Martin Radowill
Executive Director

P.S. Because charitable contributions are tax deductible, your contribution to West Park costs less than you think. For example: A $100 contribution by a person in the 30 percent tax bracket actually costs only $70! How come? Because, if the contribution wasn't given, the donor would have paid $30 additional tax to the government. Instead, you get to keep it. Or you can use it to increase your contribution. The donor in the above example actually could increase the amount of the contribution to $143 and still have it cost less than $100. Whichever you do, the important point to remember is: Make a contribution to West Park and save the tax. It's that simple ... and that worthwhile. Why don't you save some taxes today.

YOUR HELP IS NEEDED IN BUILDING WEST PARK

Letter Overcomes Deficit

This letter was used in this past year to help our agency overcome a deficit. We had more than a 50% response and that does not include those who called offering volunteer services in addition to or in lieu of money. In this letter we were able to appeal to those who had actually experienced our service at a time of trauma in their lives. We involved the prospective donors by coming back to them with many of the same words they had previously used in thanking us for our service.

Prior to this, we had approached these same people with professional brochures showing all of our wonderful services and asked them to contribute assuring them of a tax break because of their generosity. That appeal had very little success, but the response to the letter "appealing to the heart" rather than "the pocketbook" was overwhelming. We not only received gifts from the people to whom the letter was addressed, but from their families and friends.

With so many organizations asking for money these days, it is extremely important to present your cause in a positive framework that will pique the interest of the probable donor.

Bonnie Marie Leib

Home Health Care™
A non-profit corp.

11701 Shaker Boulevard • Cleveland, Ohio 44120 • 216/229-9090

ROSEMARY A. PAUL
Executive Director

April 2, 1984

Dear Friend of Hospice:

> "It would be hard to put words on paper that could express my thanks to your entire staff. As you know my husband passed away after an extensive illness. I think it is truly remarkable that I can look back and say what wonderful and loving care he received from the Home Health Care staff. Frankly, I don't know what we would have done without your help. The compassion shown will never be forgotten by myself or my family. We were given firm support, practical advice, and a sense of someone professionl always backing us up, all with tender caring."

The excerpt above is a combination of sentiments expressed by people who were served by the Home Health Care Hospice Team. Perhaps you, too, can remember having feelings such as this--"Frankly, I don't know what we would have done without your help."

The Hospice Program of Home Health Care is now in need of your help. Many of the services provided through the Home Health Care Hospice Program are not covered by any kind of insurance. We feel that without the complete progam, our ability to give the total support desired by the Hospice patient and their family is severely hampered. Therefore, we are seeking funding from other sources.

Home Health Care, a charitable organization, welcomes contributions which are deductible from your federal income tax.

You, who have been served by us, are the most likely to understand our needs and our value. If you are in a position to be of assistance to us, please send a donation in the enclosed self-addressed envelope. Every little bit will help us keep the program going. We are vitally concerned with meeting the needs of the community for health care in the home. We want people like you to be able to continue to say,

> "To have my brother at home, caring for him in a familiar and loving atmosphere meant so much to us and to him. With the Home Health Care staff to help us, we find a measure of solace in knowing that everything possible was done to give dignity to his journey from life to death. God Bless You Everyone!"

Please help us today if you can. Thank you!

Sincerely,

Rosemary Paul

Rosemary Paul
Executive Director

A True Story

The letter presents a true story, a fundamental human drama that is told simply, with only the "telling" details presented. The names were not changed so the family was consulted and had final approval on what was mailed. The readers learned of the struggles, the fears, the hopes and finally the death of a loved one experienced by this family. Throughout the letter, the reader is drawn into the story because of the experiences so many can share and relate to. The role that the Hospice played is presented only when it is natural. A case for support is developed through the story, not by telling the reader that they must give. If the story touches a prospective donor, they will give and give freely.

And give they did. When mailed to current donors, this letter received a 16.9% response with an average gift of $94.00. When mailed to prospects and centers of influence, it received a 6.8% response with an average gift of approximately $34.00.

In addition, we received numerous requests from donors to send copies of the letter to friends and relatives. About 40% of these people responded with gifts between $10.00 and $15.00.

Kenneth I. Menefee

Fort Sanders
Regional Medical Center | Hospice

1901 Clinch Avenue, S.W.
Knoxville, Tennessee 37916

December 1981

"Your mother is very, very sick. She is going to die. She is not going to get any better. . ."

Dear Friend:

As Beverly left her home in early March 1981, she knew she would never return. This would be her final stay in the Hospital. Beverly, at age 32, had cancer.

Beverly Rector and her husband, David, an executive with a Knoxville bank, knew this time would come. They had been preparing themselves since early January when Beverly began receiving care from the Fort Sanders Hospice team. The hardest part had been trying to prepare two young children, Melissa, age 8, and Brian, age 5, for what was to come.

A few years earlier Beverly developed breast cancer and had a mastectomy. She was undergoing reconstructive surgery when a cough developed. Tests showed that cancer had spread to her lungs. On January 7, 1981, Beverly Fraker Rector was admitted to the Hospice Program.

"Hospice" is a fairly new idea, but a concept dating to medieval times when people spoke of death surrounded by family and friends as "The Good Death." In the Middle Ages, a hospice was a waystation for weary travelers. Today, Hospice incorporates both concepts. A hospice to prepare individuals and family for "The Good Death" in a comfortable and familiar environment, became a reality in Knoxville a few years ago when Fort Sanders introduced the first Hospice Program in Tennessee.

In January, Beverly received chemotherapy at Fort Sanders. When she went home, the Hospice team helped get a hospital bed and other necessary equipment to ensure that she would be as comfortable and pain-free as possible.

By late January, Beverly was at home and able to take care of herself and her family. Friends and other family members helped out by bringing in meals and helping with the household. The Hospice nurses checked in often. Life was fairly normal.

In mid-February, Beverly was readmitted to Fort Sanders with breathing problems and had to go on oxygen. She felt weak and was withdrawn. It was during this stay in the Hospital that Beverly, with the support of her family and the Hospice team, came to terms with her own death, quietly and privately.

She improved and again went home but now needed around-the-clock care, which was provided by her husband and her mother along with assistance from Hospice nurses, Nancy Kerr and Beth Santella.

Through the encouragement of the Hospice team, Beverly and David's concerns were verbalized and discussed. The children needed to be prepared, and Beverly was concerned with leaving Melissa and Brian, never seeing them grow up.

Also heavy on her mind was that her children might someday have another mother. This was perhaps the most difficult reality for her to accept. But, again privately working this out, she later expressed her confidence that whomever David might select as a future wife would be good to her children. God had helped her while growing up, she said, and she knew that He would help her children, too.

David and Beverly, along with the Hospice nurses, tried to keep family life as normal as possible and involve Melissa and Brian, in their mother's care. Melissa would help by tearing tape when Beverly needed an I.V., and Brian would pat her hand, fluff her pillow and do whatever he could. The children were able to give and receive comfort. Often they would climb up in bed and play games or put on a show. Just spending time together was important.

Nancy and Beth were able to control the symptoms and pain so Beverly could enjoy her time at home with her family. She often expressed her desire to be able to die in her sleep, easily, and quietly.

In a few weeks Beverly began to get worse. She asked to go back to Fort Sanders.

On March 6, 7 and 8, David and Hospice nurse, Beth Santella, had many conversations about how to prepare the children, and to tell them that death was permanent—their mother was not coming home from the Hospital this time. They discussed his feelings about what the children should know, his new role in the family, and the changes that would take place in his life.

David brought Melissa and Brian to the Hospital and, in a secluded conference room, told them, "You know, your mother is very, very sick. She is

Fort Sanders
Regional Medical Center | Hospice
1901 Clinch Avenue, S.W.
Knoxville, Tennessee 37916

going to die. She is not going to get any better. She is going to die." Their conversation continued for many minutes, David answering their questions. He then asked if they would like to see their mother.

As Melissa came into the room, she patted Beverly's hand, went to a window, climbed on a chair, and stared out. David took little Brian downstairs. Beverly looked at Melissa and asked, "Do you want to lie down with me?" "Yes, Mommie," she replied. As they lay looking at each other, Melissa asked, "You're not going to get any better, are you?" "No, but I'm okay right now."

On March 13, 1981, David and Beverly's mother were asleep by her bedside. In the pre-dawn hours of the morning, Beverly Fraker Rector quietly and peacefully died, as she had wanted, having come to terms with death.

Although David had prepared himself for this moment, the most difficult time of Beverly's illness came when he had to tell his two young children that their mother had died.

Several weeks after the funeral, a letter was discovered in the overnight bag that Beverly always kept packed ready for the Hospital. It was her "goodbye" letter to her husband, her children and her family.

The letter continued by saying how much she loved and was proud of Melissa and Brian. She expressed her feelings and anticipated theirs.

For some, the realization of death comes hard; for others, it never comes. But, all working with the Hospice team know there are people who care, who are concerned, who will listen, and who can be depended upon.

The story of Beverly, David, Melissa and Brian Rector is just one of the hundreds of cases that Nancy and Beth have worked on over the years. No two are ever the same.

Please join us in our efforts to continue to provide this vital and unique service to those individuals who have such a desperate need by sending your tax deductible gift to the Fort Sanders Hospital Foundation today.

Hospice deals with death, but it is as big as life, helping ensure that as many terminally ill people as possible will live the remainder of their lives, pain free and as normally and happily as possible. Fort Sanders provides the Hospice Program to the community without charge!

Fort Sanders
Regional Medical Center | Hospice
1901 Clinch Avenue, S.W.
Knoxville, Tennessee 37916

Your gift of $1,000, $500, $100, $20 or even $10 can help assure that this program will be able to continue, expand, and provide this loving care to all who need it.

In this joyous Holiday season, think of the many people who are spending this Christmas without their loved ones or who know that they may be spending next Christmas alone.

You can help ease the pain and bring comfort to others. Use the enclosed, postage-paid envelope to mail your gift today.

Thank you and may you have a very joyous and happy Holiday season.

Sincerely,

T. W. Newland
President

P. S. Please mark the appropriate box on the enclosed envelope to designate your gift to the Fort Sanders Hospice Program or to the Fort Sanders Cancer Center.

Metamorphosis.

For the butterfly, it is a beautiful and natural experience. It means transition from the confining life of a slow and ugly caterpiller to soaring freedom as a magnificent, brilliant butterfly.

Humans also experience a type of metamorphosis. Death is as natural as the transformation of the butterfly. As natural as birth. Yet too often it evokes fear, rage, and denial, rather than calm, if reluctant, acceptance on the part of those soon to encounter it.

The dying can learn to make death a peaceful and constructive experience for themselves and for their families.

And friends and loved ones left behind can learn to release their hold on those who have died. To mourn, to remember, then to go on living. In the words of Thomas Fuller, "To weep excessively for the dead is to affront the living."

Colleges and Universities

Taking Advantage Of Publicity

On January 17, 1984, The New York Times front page carried an article titled "Berkeley Tops Scholars' Rankings of Graduate Schools' Reputations." The article stated "The University of California at Berkeley emerged as the strongest graduate institution across the board on a 'reputational' scale in which faculty members rated the academic quality of their peers across the country." This was the impetus for the mailing dated March 9, 1984. The message was timely in view of the fact that state papers simultaneously carried the message that fees were to be raised again at Berkeley to meet the State's fiscal crisis.

To add credibility to the mailing, articles from The New York Times, Time, the Los Angeles Times and San Francisco Chronicle were reprinted and included with the letter.

The message was clear. Private support was critical to maintain the excellent rankings. The letter asked for **$100** to match the surcharge of $100 on the students. Our results were remarkable. Over $180,000 from 2,600 was raised within 8 weeks.

I believe the success was due to the timeliness and the fact that the public was aware of our need; we were not fabricating the need.

To this date no subsequent piece has yielded the same results.

Susan M. Collins

UNIVERSITY OF CALIFORNIA, BERKELEY

BERKELEY • DAVIS • IRVINE • LOS ANGELES • RIVERSIDE • SAN DIEGO • SAN FRANCISCO SANTA BARBARA • SANTA CRUZ

OFFICE OF THE CHANCELLOR BERKELEY, CALIFORNIA 94720

March 9, 1983

Dear Friend,

January 17 was a proud day for the University and its alumni and friends.

"The University of California in Berkeley emerged as the strongest graduate university by scholars across the board," announced The New York Times' front page.

For the third time in 16 years, Cal was judged the nation's foremost graduate university by scholars across the country. In fact our standing grew stronger, moving from a tie for highest ranking in 1966 to a clear lead now.

The strength of Berkeley is a tribute first of all to its faculty and their teaching (which includes undergraduates) and research. Cal's staff played a key role in that, too.

It may well be, however, that it was the rising commitment by alumni and friends of Berkeley which provided for much of our gain. Those extra resources given during the past 10 years sustained our momentum during difficult times.

The news of Cal's ranking came as we met to decide how the University could reduce expenditures by $5 million in five months as a result of the State's fiscal crisis. By not buying library books for five months, or teaching equipment, and by deferring the repair of buildings, we will save $2 million. Another $500,000 must come from departments, even though some were cut earlier this year.

The remaining $2.5 million will be offset by a $100 surcharge added to every student's fee in the spring.

So students are hit twice by the State's fiscal crisis: by the surcharge, and by the loss of books and equipment. We must have the $100 surcharge to meet the State budget requirement. The books and equipment are another matter. We can do something about them.

If you will match the surcharge for one or more students, I will use the money to buy the books and equipment. With this special gift, you can make a difference in a very special way . . . by matching our students.

Help sustain Cal's ranking as the nation's foremost university. Your gift will ease some of the burden on our students. Thank you for considering this special request.

With best wishes for 1983

Ira Michael Heyman
Chancellor

New Approach Improves Bequest Results

This letter was part of a package recently sent to selected alumni of the arts and sciences at New York University, with the aim of raising our level of bequest giving. The campaign followed a similar, successful drive to enroll more gift annuitants in our planned giving programs.

In the past, letters for this purpose have gone to alumni over the signatures of deans, alumni organization officers, or other officials of the University. With this series, we sought to do away with the brisk formality that had prevailed and to create in its place a tone which would evoke a warm, nostalgic response in our alumni—and, we hoped, nudge them into making bequests.

Therefore, we decided on a new approach. We recruited several current alumni donors, of whom Ms. C is one, to represent the University to their classmates. In letters which they signed, they recalled their days at NYU and endorsed bequest giving as an effective means for helping the University perpetuate its tradition of excellence. A brochure on bequests, also attached, was included with each letter.

The letter went out on June 9th of this year. We have been receiving responses for only two weeks. However, even in this limited time, we have seen evidence of the success of the effort, as all but one respondee has advised us that **NYU is in his or her will.** We couldn't ask for more than that. We anticipate continued success with the program and plan to extend it to other areas of planned giving over the next year.

Pauline Chapman
Jane Savitt Tennen

Margaret L. Carulli
New York, N.Y.

Spring 1984

Dear Fellow Graduate:

The 1940's were challenging times. They were the war years when, like many of my generation, I wanted to attend college as a full-time student but could not afford to do so. Of course, my dream seemed unrealistic because the money was scarce and I had to work. However, New York University offered me a special opportunity--the chance to achieve my dreams of a college degree by attending evening classes at Washington Square College.

In those days, NYU already had a reputation as a large, bustling city university. I wondered what going to night school would be like. Would there be a sense of community? Would the faculty be good? Would we be considered a part of the University community? I needn't have worried.

The names come flooding back: Rudolph Kagey; Dr. Lillian Herlands Hornstein; Professor John Terry, the authority on Thomas Wolfe; all of them offering the "delights" of civilization. What is more, the sense of family and the warmth and understanding of all concerned were a surprise and a delight at this great urban center. In all, my years as an NYU night student were among the most rewarding of my life.

Whether we attended as day or night students, graduate or undergraduate, New York University gave us all something very special--the chance to be part of a great tradition of learning and achievement, regardless of our ethnic or economic backgrounds. I can honestly say that I would not be where I am today, running my own business, without the excellent educational foundation I received at NYU.

Now I feel it is my turn to give something back. I want to make sure that NYU--the largest private university in the country--can continue its tradition of educating students without regard to financial need. This is one of its greatest strengths.

I hope that you, too, will also consider a bequest to NYU. Please take a moment to read the enclosed brochure. It answers questions many of us have about bequests and includes a form that you can send back for more complete information with no obligation.

With a bequest to New York University, you can join me in helping to ensure that students tomorrow will enjoy the same educational opportunities that meant so much to us.

Sincerely,

Margaret L. Carulli

Margaret Carulli
Class of 1947
Washington Square College

Three Purposes For This Letter

We wanted to 1) thank our donors of $100 or more; 2) get them thinking about next year; and 3) get them to give more next year by using our Pre-Authorized Monthly Giving Program. So, I wrote this letter.

Incidentally, the reference to soap-free water has to do with the fact that our students often put soap in our pretty fountain area.

Jack F. Fortes

Stetson University

Campus Box 8279
DeLand, Florida 32720
(904) 734-4121, Ext. 344

May 7, 1984

Dear Mr. Adams:

Danke Schoen! Merci! Gracias! In three languages plus our own (Thank you!), Stetson wants to express appreciation for your generous support during the 1983-84 year, which closes this month.

Looking ahead, you may be interested in a new program that will make it possible (perhaps even more convenient) for you to give at approximately the same level in the 1984-85 year, or to advance to a new gift club.

With our new Pre-Authorized Giving plan, you can start in June with a monthly deduction that will mean:

--Receiving no more appeals from Stetson.

--Having your gift automatically sent to Stetson.

--Satisfying your need to continue supporting a worthy institution, one in which you have already made generous investments, and

--Helping Stetson in a way far greater than you thought possible.

In return, Stetson wants to send you something you would like to have in the way of a campus memento--within reason, of course! Tell us if you want a sketch of a certain building, a special photo, a vial of soap-free water from Holler Fountain--whatever. We'll try our best to comply--a personal "from Stetson to you" response.

Just complete the enclosed card and return it as soon as possible. Then we'll try to find more ways to say, "Thank you."

Sincerely,

Jack F. Fortes
Director of Special Gifts

JFF:srg
Enclosures

"The Response Was Overwhelming"

Since the Alumni Association Directory had not been revised for several years and it was time to do it again, why not send it as a gift in December as a part of the year-end annual funds campaign?

I composed the accompanying letter and sent it over the signature of the President of the Alumni Council. A week later we mailed the Directories along with a memo which read in part:

> Enclosed is your gift of the DDH Alumni Association Directory, as promised.I hope that you have had a chance to mail your contribution to the 1983 Alumni Fund. If not, please do so before December 31st.

The response was overwhelming. Disciples Divinity House has only 314 total alumni and the part-time development program is only a few years old, so the institution has not counted on major support from its graduates thus far. Most of them are moderately paid teachers in seminaries and universities or pastors in local churches. The dramatic increase in 1983 giving over 1982 gifts surprised everyone. Alumni increased their giving 177%! The dollar increase is still modest with such a small alumni group to start with but gifts increased from a mere $1,730 in 1982 to $4,793 in 1983. This reflected a 46% increase in the number of contributing alumni or about one-third of the total.

The success of the 1983 Alumni campaign has opened many new doors for major and deferred gift approaches. Sending the Directory as a "Christmas present" was a gimmick. It would have been sent in any case, but it just proves that you can sometimes find a development slant even in the course of routine administrative functions.

Norman A. Wells

THE DISCIPLES DIVINITY HOUSE
OF THE
UNIVERSITY OF CHICAGO
1156 EAST FIFTY-SEVENTH STREET
CHICAGO · ILLINOIS 60637
(312) 643-4411

THE ALUMNI COUNCIL

December 9, 1983

Dear Alumnus or Alumna:

If I told you that you should give a gift because you are going to receive a gift you might think me quite crass; too caught up in the commercial transactions of Christmas.

However, I am going to do just that. In a few days, each of us is going to receive a gift from the Disciples Divinity House. You will, I know, find it useful and helpful.

The gift is the brand new 1983 edition of the DDH Alumni Association Directory. The new directory is filled with information and is going to be very valuable in helping us to stay in touch with one another and in bringing us up to date on our whereabouts and vocational involvements. The cost of this project has not been insignificant in terms of research time, printing and mailing.

Yet it is coming to you without charge; as a gift!

Now about your gift to the House: DDH needs our gifts this year. The old days of surpluses and plenty are at an end. Expenses have now drawn abreast of income monies and are threatening to outpace them before the end of the current academic year.

We who were helped so generously during the times of plenty should not be reluctant to help out now in these leaner times. Last year our 1982 gifts to the Alumni Fund totaled a very modest $1,705. And this was an embarrassing decrease of $790 from our previous year's total.

This year's goal is $2,750 -- a 10% increase over our 1981 total.

To reach this goal, in support of quality theological education, more DDH alumni and alumnae are going to have to add the Disciples Divinity House to their Christmas gift list. In a few days, you will be receiving your Directory, a gift from the House. However, we all know that the real gifts from the House were given to us some time ago when we were accepted for study at the Divinity School of the University of Chicago and/or with the Federated Theological Faculty. It was then that the gifts of support, collegiality and Christian counsel were provided by the Disciples Divinity House.

These are the gifts to recall when the Alumni Association Directory arrives in your mail. And these are the gifts to recall when making your important gift to the 1983 Alumni Fund.

My very best wishes to each of you in this Holiday season.

Yours sincerely,

Ian McCrae, President, The Alumni Council

Northern Arizona University · FLAGSTAFF, ARIZONA 86011
UNIVERSITY RELATIONS AND DEVELOPMENT
BOX 4094
PHONE (602) 523-3983

Dear (employee's first name):

Welcome to the NAU family!

As you become more familiar with your new responsibilities, you may recognize some opportunities to improve the programs and services in your area, and the development office would like to know about them.

We are the fund-raising arm of the University. When we visit with our corporate and individual donors, we carry a portfolio of funding projects with us, and we would like to include your project. Simply write a one- or two-page overview of the project in a comfortable style, as if you were writing a letter to a friend, or come and chat with us about your project.

Perhaps you have some ideas on how we might be more effective in our fund-raising, or perhaps you know of someone who may be able to make a contribution to the University. We'd like to hear from you!

We ask that all fund-raising contacts be cleared through our office, so that we can coordinate all the University's development efforts. We also offer a variety of support services to faculty and staff interested in fund-raising.

Each year, the University conducts an Annual Fund Campaign, including an exciting five-hour telethon. If you would like to help with the next telethon or simply want to learn more about it, give us a call at x-2012.

As part of our Annual Fund Campaign we invite faculty and staff to make a contribution to the University. We invite you to join with other members of the NAU community in supporting the campus programs which are of most interest to you. Every nickel of your tax-deductible gift will be used for the purpose you designate. Contributions toward scholarship funds are one of the most popular forms of support among our faculty and staff. Or you may want to contribute to the general fund, in which case your support will be used wherever it is most needed.

Page 2

Many of your colleagues find it convenient to fulfill their pledges through payroll deduction. If you prefer to write a check, make it payable to the Northern Arizona University Foundation, Box 4094.

We recognize that not everyone is in a position to make a gift to NAU, and that each of our employees supports the University by giving of themselves, by speaking well of the University in the community and by steering prospective students to NAU.

Once again, welcome. You are a valued addition to the NAU family. Please let us know about the funding needs in your area, or just stop by for a visit.

Sincerely,

Paul R. Martin
Director of Development

PRM:gf

Involving New Employees

Here is a copy of our "new employee letter." The development office at NAU was established just three years ago. Most of our faculty and staff are not familiar with the mission and operations of the development office, nor are they in the habit of providing financial support and/or recommending prospective donors. The enclosed letter is one of the ways in which we address these concerns.

We have been using this letter only for the past few months. A dozen or so new employees have stopped by the office or written us in response to the letter. We have received a number of informal compliments on the letter, and no negative feedback.

Paul R. Martin

Remembered In Wills

Columbia Theological Seminary had just moved through a successful "Commitment to Excellence Capital Funds Campaign" which had exceeded its goal of $7,000,000 in the Fall of 1982. The Board of Directors and the Seminary Community were grateful for the fine support it had received from the churches, the foundations and the many individuals who had enabled the Seminary to go over the top in the Campaign.

As the Director of Development, I felt that the time was right to follow up the Campaign with a "Wills Emphasis" appeal. In planning for this effort, the Development Committee expressed an interest in trying to identify persons who were remembering Columbia Seminary in their Wills, thereby affording the President of the University an opportunity to thank them for their interest and support while they were living.

It was at this point that I designed the enclosed "mailing package" consisting of a letter, a pamphlet and response instrument.

The letter was a result of working closely with the Seminary's President Emeritus, the brochure was developed with permission of Mrs. Catherine Marshall before her death in 1983, and the response instrument provided a means for persons including the Seminary in their Wills to let the administration know about it.

As a result of this mailing to approximately 3,500 donors, we identified sixty-seven (67) persons who had decided to include Columbia Seminary in their Wills. We also had a very positive response to the mailing throughout our constituency and feel that the information it provided will be productive in the years ahead.

Richard A. Dodds

Columbia Theological Seminary

PETER MARSHALL

LEFT NO WILL

. . . BUT HIS

LEGACY LIVES ON

Dear Friends of Columbia Seminary:

During the last 155 years of the mission of Columbia Theological Seminary, over 3,400 persons have received their theological training and have given themselves to service in the Church of Jesus Christ as pastors, teachers, missionaries, chaplains, counselors, and administrators. God has richly blessed and used the graduates of Columbia Seminary over the years.

One of Columbia Seminary's most distinguished and honored graduates was Peter Marshall, Class of 1931. Dr. Marshall was recognized as one of the outstanding preachers in America in the 1930's and was called to become the Pastor of the New York Avenue Presbytérian Church of Washington, D.C., in 1937. In addition to his pastoral responsibilities, he served as the Chaplain of the United States Senate until his sudden death in 1949.

Peter Marshall's life and ministry are well documented in the remarkable best-selling book, "A Man Called Peter," written by his wife Catherine. The book was made into a movie and proved to be a powerful witness to the Gospel through the sermons of Peter preached in the film. The book and the film were used to challenge many persons, who seldom attended church, to consider the claims of Christ.

Peter Marshall, as a young Scotsman, first came to Columbia Seminary in the Fall of 1928 with a scholarship provided by the Men's Bible Class of the First Presbyterian Church of Birmingham, Alabama. Soon after coming to Columbia Seminary to serve as President in 1932, I had frequent contacts with Peter while he served his first pastorate in nearby Covington, Georgia. His energy and zest for life and for the ministry of the Church of Jesus Christ seemed inexhaustible. With a winsome Scottish brogue and an ability to paint word pictures and preach the Gospel with imagination and power, Peter Marshall became a highly respected and widely quoted "Preacher of the Word."

His untimely death in 1949 was a source of distress to all who knew and loved him. In a book, "To Live Again," written by Mrs. Marshall in 1957, she devoted several paragraphs to the subject of wills that began with the words, "Peter--to the surprise of all who had known him--had left no will." These words have been reproduced in pamphlet form and widely distributed (see enclosure).

When Catherine Marshall was asked about using this material in connection with the Peter Marshall Chair of Homiletics and other possible gifts to Columbia Theological Seminary, she shared her reluctance over the commercialization that has for so many years attended the use of these paragraphs by various business organizations and told us that the Seminary was one of the few places where she would allow these thoughts to be used.

Mrs. Marshall's willingness to address the matter of the importance of a will has proven helpful to countless numbers of persons and encouraged them to avoid unnecessary legal entanglements and expensive probate costs in the settlement of estates.

Although Peter Marshall left no will, his legacy lives on. His legacy lives on through the Peter Marshall Chair of Homiletics at Columbia Seminary established by his family, alumni/ae and friends. Dr. Wade P. Huie, the present Peter Marshall Professor of Homiletics, seeks to instill within the student body of Columbia, a recognition of the centrality of preaching and a love for the proclamation of the Word. The legacy of Peter Marshall lives on.

As you make plans to prepare a will or possibly review and revise your present will, I ask that you consider Columbia Theological Seminary as a channel for honoring the Lord and forwarding the aims of His Kingdom through your last will and testament.

Your bequest could be an investment in the future ministry of the Church by providing much-needed financial aid for deserving students. Your bequest could also be the means of touching the lives of countless numbers of people for Christ for generations to come . . . and the legacy of the proclamation of the Word of God will live on.

It is my hope that you will give this request your thoughtful and prayerful consideration. If you have already included Columbia Seminary in your will, you may wish to write to President J. Davison Philips to inform him so the Seminary can say "thank you" now.

With every good wish, I am

Sincerely yours,

J. McD. Richards

J. McDowell Richards
President Emeritus

P.S. A series of helpful booklets on the subject of "A Better Financial Future For You" is available through our Office of Development. Simply check the enclosed Confidential Request Card and send it to the Seminary in the envelope provided. Thank you.

JMcR/d
Enclosures

CONFIDENTIAL

Dear President Philips:

☐ This is to inform you that I/we have already made provision for COLUMBIA THEOLOGICAL SEMINARY in my will.

☐ I/We are making plans to include COLUMBIA THEOLOGICAL SEMINARY in my will

Signature ______________________________

REQUEST

Please send information on the topics indicated below:

☐ A Will to Express Your Wishes

☐ Gifts in Trust

☐ Gifts of Life Insurance

☐ Plans that Meet Women's Goals

☐ Gifts of Real Estate

☐ Gift Annuities

☐ Gifts Made Outright Now

A 303% Increase

I am enclosing a sample of what I think is a good letter and package that did work.

The letter contained the various aspects of a good solicitation piece, that is:

1. Gave a purpose and a deadline.

2. Incorporated a theme, timeliness, and an incentive.

3. Introduced a new concept—the challenge grant.

4. Was a complete package—appeal, response card, and return envelope.

This mailing resulted in a 303% increase in the number of gifts received and a 257% increase in dollars received. These figures are in comparison to the prior year's fall mailing.

All qualifying donors received a share of stock (copy enclosed) to which we applied an embossed foil seal and entered the person's name. The purpose of the "stock" was to make the person feel like an "owner" of the college and to reinforce the idea that he has a financial responsibility to the institution. (As a State institution, this was a new concept, i.e., financial responsiblity for our alumni.)

Thank you for the opportunity to share ideas.

William J. Sutton

The Kutztown College Foundation

Administration Building, Room 222
Kutztown State College
Kutztown, PA 19530

Dear Alumni and Friends:

The Annual Fund Committee wishes you could have been present for our last meeting at which time it was announced that WE have a CHALLENGE! ! !

Several Alumni and Non-Alumni special friends of Kutztown State College are providing a special CHALLENGE GRANT to the College Foundation. These anonymous friends will contribute $1 for every $2 of "new money" given to the Foundation between now and December 31st. (Limit of $10,000). New money is defined as gifts from persons who did not contribute last year and as gifts over and above what a donor gave last year. We **must** receive the gifts given last year **plus** $10,000 in new gifts before the end of the year. All gifts will be applied toward the 1982-83 goal of $90,000.00.

In 1980-81 – the $55,000 goal was met
In 1981-82 – the $65,000 goal was exceeded
In 1982-83 – our goal is $90,000 + challenge gift

Your support of your alma mater is needed NOW more than ever before to help insure the continued growth and excellence of the College. I have been associated with the College since 1912 and have always known it to successfully meet its challenges with the help of its Alumni and friends. As you read the enclosed brochure, I ask that you consider a gift to help us meet this present Challenge.

We are calling this year's effort the "Commitment Campaign". The few, anonymous donors have demonstrated their commitment to Kutztown State College and they are challenging your commitment. The College has a proud heritage and a brighter future with your help and support.

Please make an investment in the future of Kutztown State College by providing a gift to this Challenge.

Sincerely yours,

Mary E. Rickenbach

Miss Mary Rickenbach '12
(Former Dean of Women)
Honorary Chairperson
1982-83 "Commitment Campaign"

"That the future may benefit from our actions today."

Keystone State Normal School

1866

Be it known that ______ holds title to One Share of stock in Keystone State Normal School located in the Borough of Kutztown within the Commonwealth of Pennsylvania. The bearer of this stock demonstrates belief in the need, value and purpose of public education.

SIGNED ______

FEBRUARY 10, 1866

Schools

A Gain Of 40 Per Cent

This letter was sent by members of the Board of Directors to approximately 800 friends and acquaintances. Each letter was personally addressed, and each solicitor signed his/her own letters. Accompanying each letter was a contribution envelope, as well as an attractive brochure describing the organization. The results were excellent, and individual contributions increased almost 40% over the previous year.

We believe that the letter brought results because it succinctly describes our program and our needs. The opening quote, written by an 8-year-old student, tells what music can mean to a child. By using her as a typical example of the population whom we serve (musically gifted youngsters from low-income families), we made the description of our services very human and personal.

Because we believe that potential contributors want to know what their dollars produce, we boasted of the achievements of our graduating students. The need was clearly defined to the prospect by citing the percentage of the budget that must come from private sources.

The repetition of the last sentence of the quote emphasizes the valuable side-effects of musical training, especially for those living in the inner-city.

The letter was brief and easily read. It captured the reader's attention immediately, and surprised him with the fact that the writer of the quote was only eight years old. We received many favorable comments on the letter, and, of course, the best result was the large number of new contributors to the organization, plus the wonderful amount of much-needed money that we collected.

Alice S. Pfaelzer

THE MERIT PROGRAM, INC.

MUSIC EDUCATION REACHING INSTRUMENTAL TALENTS

November 16, 1983

Mr. & Mrs. John Jones
1234 Any Street
Chicago Illinois 60600

Dear Mary and John:

"Music is one of the cures for frustration. It relaxes the mind and it also calms the soul. Music is a wonderful medicine. Listening to music has inspired me to play the piano and to learn to write my own songs. Music has a sort of magic that is like a soft breeze. ...Music is like a warm friendly welcome to me. It is no wonder that music is called food for the soul. Music opens up many doors to cure frustrations."

The above was written by a student, aged 8, in The Merit Program. Because of our unique Tuition-Free Conservatory, this young musician is able to pursue her quest for musical knowledge, despite the fact that she comes from a family whose annual income is less than $8,000. At The Merit Program, Kharma receives weekly instruction in cello and theory. She is typical of the 200 students enrolled in our Saturday programs. She, as all students in MERIT, was selected by audition. She was then placed in one of our two Divisions (Preparatory or Advanced) for her weekly classes.

Because of the comprehensive, high quality training which MERIT provides, its graduates are able to go on to college, most on scholarships. MERIT proudly takes credit for having helped to obtain over $50,000 in college scholarships for its class of 1983. MERIT's 27-member faculty are professional musicians and teachers. They provide the highest quality music instruction available, as well as the guidance and counseling which our students so desperately need. Because these services are extremely expensive, each year MERIT must raise at least 75% of its budget from grants and contributions.

As one who is vitally interested in helping these young people, I am writing to ask you to join me in assuring a future for them. Your contribution to The Merit Program, Inc. will indeed "open up many doors to cure frustrations."

Thank you for your generosity.

Sincerely,

Roger Weiss
President

Alice S. Pfaelzer, Executive Director/ Emma Endres-Kountz, Program Director Emeritus
410 South Michigan Avenue, Suite 710, Chicago, Illinois 60605, 312/786-9428

Telling It Like It Is

This direct mail letter hit home. For the first time parents were told that the tuition they paid for their children was **not** the cost of the education their children were receiving. Most parents were shocked.

The numbers on the side of the page added up to the actual total goal. People like to have choices. Each parent was given three options for the designation of their gift.

The response was overwhelming. This letter raised over $100,000, which was $40,000 more than had ever been raised in a direct mail campaign in the past 33 years.

The most important ingredient was: telling it like it is . . . the truth.

Bonnie S. Hyra

BCS
INTEGRATING
FAITH
and LEARNING

"Trust in the Lord with all your heart and lean not on your own understanding; in all your ways acknowledge Him, and He will direct your paths." Proverbs 3:5-6

November 22, 1983

Dear BCS Parent,

There are 875 students on scholarship at BCS this year.

Are you aware that the tuition paid for each student does not cover the actual cost of educating that student? The difference between tuition and the actual cost of education is an average of $210 per student.

$25,000

What that means, in simple terms, is that each student at BCS is being partially supported by the financial gifts of people like you and me. Of the total goal for this December Giving campaign, $25,000 will go into the GENERAL OPERATING FUND to fill that gap.

A high priority of the BCS Board of Directors is to make BCS affordable for all Christian parents who desire it for their children, regardless of financial status. That is why the board has held tuition costs as low as possible. But some families need financial assistance beyond that.

$50,000

There are 38 families at BCS this year whose students could not be here at all if it were not for generous gifts to the BCS SCHOLARSHIP FUND. Unfortunately, that fund is almost dry. We are counting on $50,000 from this December Giving campaign to provide for these scholarships, which have already been promised.

The eight volunteers who make up the BCS Board are parents with children in the school. We are concerned not only with finances, but also with how our finances are used to strengthen the academic program and improve the facilities.

$25,000

We are pleased to see campus improvements, such as the newly finished home economics room, which contribute to the quality of education at BCS. Of the December Giving campaign, $25,000 will be designated for SPECIAL PROJECTS FUND.

This is an exciting time for BCS. We are seeing the need to consider some expansion. YOU can be a partner in the vision the Lord has for BCS. Please use the enclosed bookmark to remind you of our prayer needs. Consider sending a gift today.

Sincerely,

Al Erisman

Al Erisman, Chairman
BCS School Board

$100,000

P.S. Thank you for your help. Please use the enclosed envelope and card to return your year-end gift towards our $100,000 goal.

Bellevue Christian School

Main Campus • Preschool, Kindergarten, Grades 7-12 | Three Points Campus • Grades 1-6
1601 98th Avenue N.E. • Bellevue, Washington 98004 • 454-4028 | 7800 N.E. 28th Street • Bellevue, Washington 98004 • 454-397

An Increase Of $18,000

I like this particular letter for several reasons, the main one being that it caused much comment but also because it got results. The letter was sent to all 1600 people on the mailing list and helped bring up our total from $51,000 to $73,000. It was followed up with personal contacts and a phonathon, so it was not used exclusively. However, it was a major part of the campaign.

I also like the letter because it gets the attention of the reader with a human interest story, which is a combination of two comments made during a conversation about the "old days." Dramatic contrast is used to compare how things have gone up—tuition is now $2200 and these people knew it from previous publications. We also emphasized our positive points, told where the money goes, and then made our appeal.

Margaret N. Kelley

Bright School

Telephone 615/267-8546

Hixson Pike
Chattanooga, Tennessee 37405

Dear Friend of Bright School,

A friend told me, "Not long ago, my mother gave me a little cardboard box filled with report cards, notes, and, most interesting to me now, the bills she and my dad paid for me to attend Bright School. Hey, back in the '40s, it cost less than $200. Isn't it amazing how times have changed?" But then he added, "I also remember the year I learned my father made $10,000. I thought we were rich. That's amazing, too. Now $10,000 probably won't send my child to college for a year."

You may think like my friend and be shocked how things have gone up, especially the good things in life, like a superior education -- and salaries, including those of teachers. Even though they make less than teachers in the public system, our teachers receive almost 70% of our budgeted income. If we want to keep our outstanding teachers and attract others when needed, we have to figure that amount will continue to increase.

What about our programs at Bright School? We spend a portion of the budget each year to keep our teachers trained and informed about updated subject matter and teaching methods. That's vital in maintaining our position of excellence in elementary education. And then there are books, supplies, and upkeep of our marvelous facility that some generous people before us saw fit to build. We take pride in providing excellent food. We have wonderful "food for the soul," too, in our music and arts program, and don't forget the practical program of manual arts, unique in our city. There is no extra charge for building character!

So when you really give it some thought, we are getting an excellent return for our money at Bright School. Since it takes more than tuition, we supplement the budget each year with the Annual Sustaining Fund Drive. During the drive, we ask all of you who care about Bright School and are a part of its ongoing tradition, and who have a desire to insure its future, to provide approximately 10% of our budget through tax-deductible gifts to the school. It is so important in order for us to preserve and enhance what we already have. And you are so important in making that happen.

Last year we exceeded our goal and so we gave ourselves -- and you -- a Blue Ribbon for Excellence. This year we want to raise $70,000. Won't you consider helping us "come in first" again?

Sincerely,

Peggy (Mrs. William A.) White
General Chairman

"Charge Card" Pays Off

Persuasive letters of a religious nature have a long history. Many of the Biblical epistles are persuasive in tone. Some of the writings of religious leaders such as St. Augustine, Justinian, and Martin Luther were intended to persuade people to responsible action.

Today's religious leaders produce a plethora of written persuasion, including many types of fund raising letters. This presents quite a challenge to the development officer of a small religious organization, who must somehow capture the reader's attention and inspire an act of stewardship.

The CHARGE CARD letter met this challenge during the Christmas campaign of 1983. Attached to the school's masthead was a card stock Master Card replica, with the words: "Give Christ charge of your life." The letter succeeded because it was:

Cost Effective: It brought a response of 21 percent, with an average gift of $550.35 and an average cost of 65 cents per letter.

Current: Charge cards are popular items around Christmas time.

Fresh: The copy referred to familiar Bible passages in new and ironic perspectives.

Direct: The letter boldly asked for a gift of $1,000 (from donors who had previously given at least that much during a year.)

Personal: Each copy of the letter was individually typed on a letter-quality word processor, and personally signed.

Dr. John J. Komar

LOS ANGELES LUTHERAN HIGH SCHOOL

Telephones—
L.A. (213) 875-1634
Valley (213) 768-2616

7500 N. Glenoaks Blvd.
Burbank, Calif. 91504

Christmas, 1983

Mr. and Mrs. John Smith
22451 Wedgewood Avenue
Los Angeles, CA 90022

Dear Mr. and Mrs. Smith:

Our Lord and Savior Jesus Christ wants you to live abundantly (John 10:10). So I've enclosed a CHARGE CARD to help you to do that.

This is a special kind of CHARGE CARD, with unique advantages:

> You'll never receive a bill from it. The total price was paid long ago.
>
> This CHARGE CARD has no expiration date. It's yours for eternity.
>
> Your line of credit is limitless and approved by God, Himself.

To use this CHARGE CARD, however, you must present your total being as a living sacrifice, holy and acceptable to God (Romans 12:1).

Of course, you know what sacrifice is all about. You've given as much as $1,000 in a single year to Lutheran High. This kind of stewardship has been the lifeblood of our ministry.

That's why I'm asking you to match your previous annual gift, as a Christmas present to the 535 students who are counting on the continuation of Lutheran High.

Can I count on you for $1,000? That's my prayer. Please make it yours, too. Remember--you can "charge" it.

In His service,

Ed Krueger

Rev. Ed Krueger
Coordinator of Ministries

Two Letters Bring Success

The first letter, dated December, 1982, is a simple announcement of the project and an invitation exemplary in its simplicity and efficiency of communication. Its effect was to produce 35 contributions totaling $1,670.00 from 150 letters sent. The second letter was designed to be more motivational—to arouse those who would not respond to a simple announcement and to provide additional appeal to those who had contributed on the first solicitation. The motivational technique used was to appeal to the wish to identify with the winning tradition of the local swim team and offer the opportunity to accept some personal "ownership" of the suggested future "even greater" success of these swim teams. Out of 199 second letters sent, 31 additional contributions were received and totaled $1,378.00.

The net result was a total contribution of $3,052.00 from two solicitations. In the judgement of the members of the Booster Club (many of whom are business and management types), the project was a big success beyond expectations. The letter is being modified to use for a gymnasium scoreboard project at the present time. The second letter has received local attention as a very efficient instrument.

Norman M. Jensen, M.D.

December 29, 1982

Dear

Several people believe that the very successful Madison Memorial High School boys and girls swimming program would be greatly complemented by an electronic timing system. Such a system would add an increment of sophistication and accuracy to the already awesome traditions of hard work and dedication we have come to expect from Memorial Swimming.

A simple and good quality system without a spectator display board costs approximately $3600. The Memorial Athletic Booster Club has agreed to underwrite up to $1000 of this cost.

We ask you to make a tax deductable contribution as large as you can afford. Please make checks payable to Memorial High School Athletic Booster Club and send to Guy Ferris, 1122 Winston Drive, Madison, WI 53711; then come see the system in action at a meet. We hope to have it installed by February 1st. Thanks for your support of our student-athletes and best wishes for a great holiday season!

Sincerely,

Norm Jensen, President
Memorial Athletic Booster Club

Project Co-Sponsors:

Linda Heineke
Sal Troia
Jan and Guy Ferris
Lynda and Doug Knudson
Kay and Bob Pohle

JAMES MADISON MEMORIAL ATHLETIC BOOSTER CLUB SWIM PROJECT

March 1984

Mr. & Mrs. Norm Jensen
6210 Davenport Drive
Madison, WI 53711

Dear Mr. & Mrs. Jensen:

Now finally, we have a good timing system available for $5,000. But our previous fund-raising drive was a bit short! What to do? Much discussion! **DECISION:** Purchase the $5,000 system out of current Booster Club assets and solicit all the loyal Swim Team Boosters one more time in an effort to reduce the $3,300 burden to the Athletic Booster Club General Fund. This is the largest single expenditure for any sport in its history.

SO HERE IT COMES! What has JMM swimming meant to you? Are you proud of your association with JMM swimming excellence? Do JMM swimmers perform? Do they have fun? Are they the envy of Wisconsin? What do they take with them into life after high school? Isn't it all worth just a few more of your hard-earned dollars?

The electronic timing system will give another touch of class to an already outstanding program. Meets can be run with more accuracy and efficiency. Automatic split-time records will free coaches to observe other aspects of the race like stroke and turns. JMM can now host the Big Eight conference meet and other big meets!

If each of the JMM swim boosters contributes $10 to $30, we can totally replace the $3,300 Booster Club cost. Let's show the JMM Athletic Booster Club one important reason why swimming has achieved excellence at JMM. Let's show them how much we value this excellence.

Send $10 to $30, or as much as you can afford, to "JMM Athletic Booster Club Swim Project" and mail to treasurer Sal Troia, 7405 Farmington Way, Madison, WI 53717. Then come see the JMM swimmers in action with their new timing system. **THEY'LL MAKE YOU PROUD!**

Gratefully,

Norm Jensen

Sal Troia

Linda Heineke

Cultural Organizations

Foundation Letter Wins $75,000

This is a grant request to a local foundation that ended up netting the Bay Area Video Coalition a grant of $75,000. I think it is a good example of the classic foundation grant request letter. It is a little longer than a letter I would normally send, but we were asking for more money than usual. The main thing is—it worked!

Morrie Warshawski

BAVC

BAY AREA VIDEO COALITION

1111 17th Street
San Francisco,
California 94107
415 861-3282

Facility
861-3280

Video Networks
861-3279

August 10, 1983

Dear ___________:

As we discussed recently, the Bay Area Video Coalition (BAVC) would like to approach the XYZ Foundation for a contribution of $75,000 over a three-year period. The grant will be used as general operating support to aid us in our efforts to diversify and deliver types of video programming to the public by assisting independent videographers through our wide range of services.

BAVC was begun in 1977 as the result of a Rockefeller-funded "needs Assessment and Feasibility Study" in the Bay Area. The survey found a fertile and active community of videographers locally with a number of needs that could not be met by existing organizations (e.g. Film Arts Foundation, Video Free America, La Mamelle, Pacific Film Archives, Academy of Media and Theatre Arts, KQED, Viacom Cable, National Asian American Telecommunications Association and Optic Nerve, among others).

Since its inception BAVC has been providing all of the following services:

> Low-cost access to video cameras and post-production editing suites. BAVC is now the largest non-profit video arts center in the country. In 1982 alone we assisted over 70 projects that never could have been completed without our help. These programs have reached large audiences through: public television stations, cable television, theatres, museums, libraries and community organizations.
>
> VideoNetworks, the only newsletter on the West Coast that keeps the independent video community informed about grant deadlines, exhibition opportunities, workshops and upcoming events.
>
> Technical workshops and business seminars in all aspects of the video field.

Resource library of media arts books, magazines and videotapes.

Grant administration of worthy projects needing non-profit status.

Awards Coordination. This year we are administering "the Phelan Art Award in Video" for The San Francisco Foundation.

Our support comes from a healthy mix of earned income (which has risen from 6% in 1977 to 52% in 1982), memberships and grants (The Rockefeller Foundation, Zellerbach Family Fund, National Endowment for the Arts, Mervyn's, The San Francisco Foundation, Corporation for Public Broadcasting, Chevron, California Arts Council and others).

Our Board of Directors currently numbers five and meets on a monthly basis. The staff consists of five full-time personnel, one part-time employee, four interns and numerous volunteers. We service over 100 clients annually who represent a broad cross-section of the video community: independent video documentarians, video artists, corporate video departments, community groups, museums, hospitals, universities, libraries, non-profit arts groups, etc.

Attached is a copy of our new "Long Range Organizational Development and Stabilization Plan" just completed with the assistance of a planning grant from The San Francisco Foundation. It provides a detailed outline of the ways in which we plan to grow over the next four years. It is a direct result of close scrutiny of our programs by the community, board, staff and consultants.

The plan is characterized by a strong commitment to strengthening current programs with the steady addition of new services (e.g. distribution and residencies) and a push towards greater self-sufficiency. We project a 100% increase in our budget by 1987 with earned income representing 56% of our total revenues. The support we are requesting from your Foundation will help us maintain this type of steady, reasoned growth without jeapordizing our commitment to providing low-cost access to videographers.

The role that BAVC and independent videographers will play in the community will become ever more magnified as our society becomes increasingly based on the production and distribution of information. Video has already demonstrated its supremacy as the tool for capturing visual information and for disseminating it to the public. We are witnessing an explosion both in new outlets for visual information (e.g. cable, satellite, home video-casette recorders, etc.), in the production of programs to fill the new outlets, and in the technology for producing these programs.

BAVC is the only non-profit agency in the Bay Area currently addressing these issues with a full range of services. Without our assistance, independent videographers will not be able to afford to produce and edit non-commercial programs aimed at large audiences. They would be forced to frequent commercial post-production facilities that charge twice our rates and that offer very limited opportunities either for experimentation or training. I think it no understatement to say that the vibrancy and health of the video arts locally will be tied closely to developments here at BAVC.

Please feel free to call me for any additional information. It has been a pleasure working with you recently. I hope that you will be able to give us much needed support over the next three years.

Most sincerely,

Morrie Warshawski
Executive Director

MW/pja
Attachments

Less Calories Bring More Cash

I sent this letter to about 500 opera friends and supporters and received responses from over one-half of them. Pledges ranged from a dime to ten dollars a pound.

The results were:

It raised about $9,000.00 for the Opera Company in a good natured sort of way. None of the contributors considered this pledge to be their annual gift, and everyone enjoyed being a part of the project.

The Metro Opera received a terrific amount of publicity—two front page stories in The Des Moines Register, a New York Times piece, a National Public Radio commentary, and numerous other mentions throughout the country.

I lost 57 pounds, became healthier, and the Company's financial position was improved.

Douglas J. Duncan

Des Moines Metro
OPERA

May 3, 1983

Mr. and Mrs. Harlan Hockenberg
3920 Grand Avenue
Des Moines, Iowa 50312

Dear Harlan and Dorothy:

I need to lose weight! The opera company is always looking for funds, so, I am writing to you in the hope that you will join the "Duncan Challenge" and pledge $1.00 to the Des Moines Metro Opera for every pound I lose from April 17 until the end of the opera season on July 17. I'm shooting for fifty pounds. This "Diet for Dollars" program will fund a special children's opera performance of Cavalleria Rusticana and Pagliacci on June 28th.

Dr. Michael Richards will serve as supervisor, witness, and chief judge for this "happening" with the official weigh-in scheduled for Sunday morning, April 17, at Methodist Hospital. On July 17, we will tally up the figures and inform you of the results shortly thereafter.

Now, for my promises:

I If I gain any weight, I will donate $5.00 per gained pound to your favorite non-profit organization — yes, even the Hawkeyes!

II If I fail to take off at least 25 pounds, all pledges are off and I will personally fund the kid's program — What have I gotten myself into?

So, please help me on this quest by filling out and returning the stamped, self-addressed postcard (you may pledge more or less or nothing at all, but please send the card back) — I need all the encouragement I can get.

Just remember, this truly will be the toughest $5,000 - $7,500 I've ever raised.

Thank you.

Douglas J. Duncan, Managing Director
Des Moines Metro Opera

DES MOINES METRO OPERA, INC. - 600 NORTH BUXTON - INDIANOLA, IOWA 50125

Letter Brings Friends And Dollars

The Institute of Alaska Native Arts, a statewide not-for-profit Native Arts organization prepared and distributed a direct mail piece targeted to the readers of the Institute's bi-monthly newsletter. Establishment of a "friends" was announced in the January issue of the publication and the letter followed in February (in-between bi-monthly issues). Over 4,000 pieces were mailed along with a membership card and window envelope for return. As of May 30, 1984 (three months into the campaign) $7,000 has been received.

The letter, in addition to generating contributions, also increased awareness of the many different cultural groups served by our organization and the programs and services available.

Jean Flanagan

'nisipsiip'insk • ilaasin • yugnikek'ngat

(Tsimshian) (Aleut) (Yup'ik)

woosh een aax'w • iiliiga • gganiyoo

(Tlingit) (Inupiaq) (Koyukon)

tawlang • iilakumtag • friends

(Haida) (Siberian Yup'ik) (English)

Dear IANA Newsletter Reader

Alaska Native Culture groups - Aleut, Yupik and Inupiaq Eskimo, Athabascan, Haida, Tlingit and Tsimpshian Indians have many words meaning "friends". The logo design above translated from these languages means "people that I really like", "people that I wouldn't like parting with", "people that are together" and "friends". This describes IANA'S FRIENDS, a new and very special group you are invited to join.

You are one of over 4,000 people that the Institute of Alaska Native Arts (IANA) serves across Alaska, the "lower 48", and Europe. Our mailing list continues to grow as each eight-page bi-monthly newsletter is prepared for distribution. Your interest in Alaska Native art and the many new requests and responses we receive show interest and a firm belief in IANA's programs, services and future existence.

You receive current information on Native art and artists from IANA's newsletter. Additionally, you may have participated in IANA workshops and conferences, enjoyed our exhibits, attended other IANA sponsored programs or received technical assistance, Native art supplies, and educational materials from IANA.

IANA'S FRIENDS is a special group created to help make certain the Institute continues to maintain present standards, as well as expand when necessary, the programs and services delivered. IANA is a not-for-profit organization, and it will cost nearly half a million dollars this year to operate. When you become one of IANA'S FRIENDS your membership clearly shows us and our other funding sources that the people we serve care and want us to continue.

While your comments and ideas are always welcome at IANA, a tax-deductible contribution will truly express your support of the Institute of Alaska Native Arts. IANA'S FRIENDS receive honorable mention in our Annual Report, the IANA Newsletter and discounts on IANA publications and merchandise. A special token of our friendship will be mailed to you after we receive the enclosed card with your check or money order.

Your friendship counts at IANA!

Sincerely,

Jean Flanagan
Executive Director
Institute of Alaska Native Arts

P.O. Box 80583 • Fairbanks, Alaska 99708 • (907) 479-8473/479-4436

Membership Letter Gets Big Results

In the 24 months I was Assistant Director of Development in charge of Founders Society membership, the roll grew from 14,300 to 19,200 memberships, the vast majority of them a result of direct mail.

Creating direct mail pieces like this, based on special exhibitions or current offerings at the museum, was one of the most challenging aspects of my job. And the thrill when we received 1,100 memberships in **one month** is never to be forgotten.

I believe there is no one correct formula for successful direct mail fund raising. Advice I'd give is to read all the material the pros have to offer, gauge your audience, and 'go creative.'

Marion K. Ringe

May 1980

Please take a moment to *really* read this paragraph:

> *"Only through art can we get outside of ourselves and know another's view of the universe which is not the same as ours and see landscapes which would otherwise have remained unknown to us. . . . Thanks to art, instead of seeing a single world, our own, we see it multiply until we have before us as many worlds as there are original artists. . . . And many centuries after their core, whether we call it Rembrandt or Vermeer, is extinguished, they continue to send us their special rays."*
>
> The Maxims of Marcel Proust
> Edited and translated by
> Justin O'Brien (1948).

Coming to The Detroit Institute of Arts is more than a step through a door into a building. It is an exciting journey through a portal to a thousand landscapes, each a new and different vision of an intriguing world.

Walk into the Great Hall and feel the immensity and grandeur of ancient castles and knights of old. Step into the 17th Century American Room and experience the rough-hewn sturdiness that typified American life 300 years ago. The pulse of machinery is almost audible in Diego Rivera's powerful murals of the Ford Rouge Plant. Graceful Egyptian art; arresting Italian portraits; warm and brooding Dutch landscapes; the delicate beauty of Chinese, Japanese, and East Indian art; imaginative African masterworks; ancient, medieval, modern—all within the walls of The Detroit Institute of Arts.

The Founders Society offers you the opportunity to be more than a casual visitor to the museum. By becoming a member, you'll learn of events at the museum just for members and have privileges the general public does not have. Please turn the page for the full list of Founders benefits and a special invitation.

NEW MEMBER TOUR. Guided by our Docents, this tour will introduce the superb art collections to you.

INFORMATION ON CURRENT EVENTS. Our month-by-month Calendar will keep you up to date on exhibitions, films, lectures, concerts, and our other special events.

FREE ADMISSION TO ALL SPECIAL EXHIBITIONS. Tickets to the general public for major exhibitions are as much as $2.50 per person. As a Founder, you will be admitted free as many times as you wish. If you join at a family rate, your immediate family also will be admitted free.

OPTIONAL FREE SUBSCRIPTION TO THE *BULLETIN*. If you wish, every three months you can receive this informative collection of articles by our curators and contributing authors on museum acquisitions and other fascinating art.

FREE TICKETS TO TWO YOUTHEATRE PERFORMANCES. Enjoy two selected complimentary performances of live children's theatre.

DISCOUNTS AT OUR SHOPS. As a Founder, you save 10% on all purchases of $5.00 or more at our Museum Shops which are stocked with a fine selection of art books, posters, reproductions, crafts, jewelry and toys.

RENTAL AND PURCHASE PRIVILEGES IN OUR ART RENTAL GALLERY. You can rent by the month or buy from the largest selection anywhere of original Michigan artists.

INVITATIONS TO JOIN OUR ACTIVITIES GROUPS. We have something for everyone in our special interest groups: The Antiquaries, Associates of the American Wing, Drawing and Print Club, Friends of African Art, Friends of Asian Art, Friends of Modern Art, and Junior Council. If you're interested in becoming a Founders Society volunteer, we have a job for you that will make you a real part of your museum.

MEMBERS LOUNGE. Relax in a comfortable and inviting setting overlooking Rivera Court.

·If you decide to join at the Patron level of membership, you will also receive the following: reciprocal membership benefits in 14 other museums across the country; invitations to Patron-only events; voting privileges at the Annual Meeting held each autumn; a special gift from the Membership Office.

Although so far I have only talked about what Founders receive, your membership will be very much a *giving* experience. For through the support of your membership dues, you will be helping all of these programs:

. . . education programs in the museum, in schools and statewide through lectures and traveling exhibitions.

. . . conservation of the museum's collection.

. . . a specialized library of almost 100,000 volumes.

. . . art publications.

. . . significant acquisitions.

. . . special exhibitions brought from all over the world.

. . . application for matching funds from the National Endowment for the Arts Challenge Grant, thus providing funds to enable the museum to improve its service to you in many ways.

If you join as a new member, or renew your current membership with the enclosed application, I want to invite you to a special reception on Saturday, July 19 to see exciting new gallery installations now under construction. Please fill out the form below and the enclosed membership application, and mail them in the postage-paid reply envelope.

Thank you for your support of the Founders Society Detroit Institute of Arts.

Sincerely,

Norman B. Weston
President

Please detach and mail with your membership application card.

- -

☐ Yes, I'd like to attend the Members Reception on Saturday, July 19 at 2 p.m. Admission by ticket only. Individual members will receive two tickets. Family members please specify number desired________.

Name ____

Address ____

____

A Successful Phonathon Letter

The test of any fundraising letter is the dollars it ultimately produces, and our Phonathon Letter has consistently, over a four-year period, helped us to exceed our annual goals.

The reader's eye is immediately caught by the attractive green print on yellow paper, which is also the official colors of the Paramount. That factor, along with the use of the logo, create identification with the charitable cause even before a word is read.

"Right-to-the-point" flavor begins on the mailing envelope itself with "We'll be calling you. . ." and continues throughout the body giving the prospective donor the need, contribution mechanism, his benefits, and the importance of his contribution.

Prompt reply is encouraged by the attached pledge form, business reply envelope, and the promise that "We'll be calling you." The pledge form also suggests and provides the opportunity for the donor to make an extended pledge over several years.

Obviously, minor text changes must be made each year, but utilization of the same form promotes repeat response through familiarity.

And last, but not least, it is an honest, straight forward appeal.

Linda L. Ball

. . . . and one day very soon!

During the week of Feb. 20-24, a volunteer from the P.A.C. will be calling you to invite your participation in the 1984 "Brighter Than Ever Campaign". This year $17,000 is needed to help finance the continuation of cultural and entertainment events as well as maintain the Paramount building.

As a contributor you will receive a Certificate of Appreciation and a decal to post at your business proclaiming your community support.

If you contribute $100 or more, your name will be displayed in the Paramount lobby as a "Friend of the Arts". You will also receive two reserved tickets to The National Opera's "Elixir of Love" on April 6 at 8:00 p.m.

Your contribution is very important to the Paramount, so when your Paramount representative calls, we hope you will join us in the effort to continue making Ashland "Brighter Than Ever" and give generously to the Phonathon. Remember, all contributions are fully tax deductible.

No need to wait for our call: Mail your pledge right now!

BRIGHTER THAN EVER IN THE 80'S

Count on me to help make the Ashland Area a better place by supporting the PAC's "Brighter Than Ever in the 1980's" campaign. I pledge (circle one):

$25 $50 $100 $250 $500 Other $________

Count on my support annually for (circle one):

2 years 3 years 4 years 5 years Other________

Signature

Business name

Business address Phone

City State Zip

Detach and mail, make check payable to **Greater Ashland Foundation.**

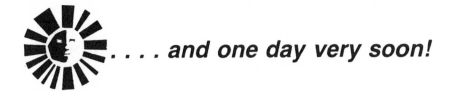

Exceeds Goal Despite Adversity

First, a little background:

The Hangar Theatre just closed its 10th summer season, our most successful to date both artistically and at the box office. We faced unusual constraints at the beginning of this year, having lost thousands of dollars of facilities and equipment provided by Cornell University in previous years. Each spring, the Hangar launches a membership drive for the purpose of raising operating funds. This drive occurs before our annual spring gala fundraiser and the season ticket campaign, usually begun at the end of April. The membership drive has been traditionally in the form of a direct mail "pitch" to a mailing list of approximately 4,000 people, a quarter of whom are previous members and season ticket holders.

In the past several years, this membership letter has been printed in brochure format, on glossy paper with lots of photographs, a coupon to clip and send and relatively few "hard facts" about the theatre's needs. We felt, given our special hardships for 1984, that we owed our members and the community a more detailed explanation of just why we needed money and needed it **now.** It also appeared to us that the type of brochure sent in the past implied a slickness and level of success that was appropriate for the artistic quality of our productions but belied the reality of our current struggle to, literally, start from scratch. Hence, the letter you see enclosed.

Has it been a success? We think so. Given the size of our community, its history of giving, both to us and to the cultural organizations of Ithaca, we set our membership goal for 1984 at $20,000.00. We had anticipated the need to do a telephone follow-up to the letter in order to achieve this goal. Due to a number of unforeseen problems which grabbed our attention that spring, we were never able to do that follow-up. Nevertheless, we exceeded our goal by $2,000.00, with contributions still coming in even though we have closed for the winter.

There's more to it than just dollars, however. This letter served as a good introduction to our situation when we made subsequent pitches, through word of mouth, public service announcements and classifieds, for donations of equipment and clothing. We started in April with not a hammer or a sewing machine to call our own and now, as we shut down the facility for the year we have a full stock of costumes, furniture and most of the tools we need to begin our 1985 season. Not a mean accomplishment!

Kathleen Henry

Hangar Theatre

MIDWINTER: A marvellous time to conjure up thoughts of a warm summer's eve and a live performance at the Hangar.

We encourage that fantasy. In a culture too frequently dominated by TV sit-coms and third-rate films, we see the Hangar as an appealing alternative.

In this letter we want to share with you some of our early plans for the 1984 season and our dreams for the future.

And, as we do each year at this time, we boldly ask you to help make it all happen again this summer. We seek your support of the Hangar Theatre through a membership contribution.

Read on, please....

Dear Theatre Lover:

1984 marks the tenth year that plays have been performed at the Hangar Theatre at Cass Park.

It was June 28, 1975 when the spell-binding opening performance of *MAN OF LA MANCHA* transformed, once and for all, a stark, cavernous hangar building into a magical space for live theatre.

Since that memorable evening the Hangar Theatre Company has given 397 performances of 32 plays. The Hangar has become an established part of summer life for a growing number of local residents and visitors.

From the beginning it has been a principal of the Hangar Board to provide a varied theatrical experience of the highest level of excellence that our always-tight budget permits.

In pursuit of this goal we have tried a number of different directions over past seasons. New programs have been developed and the range of live performance events available to the community has been broadened.

As many of you know, our operation is not always associated with light entertainment. We want to give you theatre in all it's multi-sided dimensions. We have been willing to take risks with play selections and key personnel; we have not chosen the safer and less controversial route of more commercial fare. It hasn't been an easy task.

While the results of our efforts have not always matched our hopes, your response, season after season, makes us believe there is a solid core of support for what we are trying to do.

This support takes many important forms: ticket sales, of course, but also essential and dependable contributions from our member donors--from you and others like you who see the Hangar operation as an enhancement of our community life.

LAST YEAR YOUR SUPPORT SOARED--THANK YOU!!

Last year the Hangar enjoyed support from 264 members, up from 1982. In fact, contributions have increased consistently each year since the first membership drive in 1976. Last year you donated a remarkable $18,500 with an average gift of $70.00!

If we're lucky and things go well this season, we'll need almost $20,000 in membership gifts to make income and expenses match.

This will be our third year with the same ticket prices. We are reluctant to raise prices if it means that some of our audience will be excluded. On the other hand, no ticket pays the full cost of the show it buys.

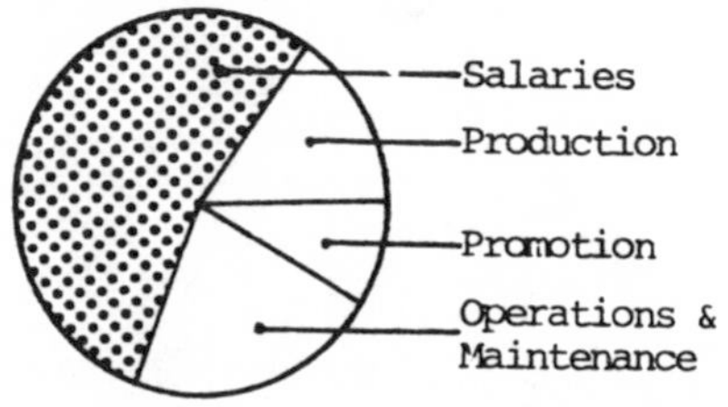

EXPENSES

Cornell, State and local agencies and foundations also hear and heed our requests. They give us money in your name, but we still need it from you directly to survive.

For the past two years, we have offered a season ticket for each contribution of $100 and we are doing so again. If you plan to buy a season ticket anyway, what a wonderful way to solve two needs with one membership check!

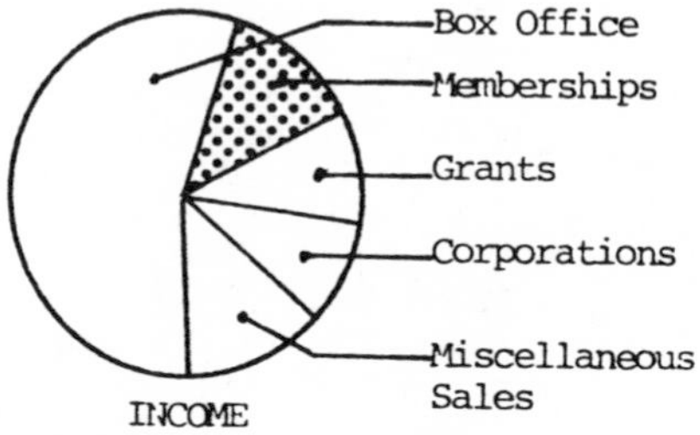

INCOME

And you help us most when we need it most -- now.

In addition....

As a 1984 Member of the Hangar, you'll receive advance mailing of the season ticket announcement, ensuring seat-selection priority at the box office. You'll be invited to special seminars with the directors and other special events during the season.

And you'll share special pride in the reputation that the Hangar is earning as one of the up-and-coming summer theatres in the State.

OUR CORNELL CONNECTION IS CHANGING -- CHALLENGES AHEAD

We are fortunate to have many talented students and faculty at Cornell and Ithaca College who are often employed as part of the Hangar Company in one capacity or another.

Cornell University continues to be extremely helpful in providing financial, administrative and moral support for our operation. But the Department of Theatre Arts at Cornell has determined that lighting equipment and shop space, so generously given in past years, will no longer be available.

We see this as both a concern and an opportunity.

A need to acquire more stage lights and space in which to build sets and costumes heads the list of concerns. Last year, for example, there were over 150 lighting instruments in the grid requiring almost a mile of cable for electrical connections.

Most of this equipment was borrowed from Cornell Theatre and will have to be found elsewhere this season.

Sets and costumes have been built in Cornell shops for the past several years. Replacement space or alternative arrangements are now being pursued -- a great financial and logistical challenge for the 1984 season and beyond.

But our cause is even greater and we are undeterred.

Cornell's Theatre Department is surely on the road to great things. A grand Performing Arts Center is coming soon and it offers the promise of making Ithaca a Mecca for the Arts.

Before too long a summer visit could include live performances at several locations in the community. The potential for a real Ithaca Theatre Festival seems enormous and such thoughts stir up great feelings of excitement.

The Hangar Theatre owes its early life to nurturing and encouragement from the schools on the hills. We look forward to developing new and fruitful relationships with both in the summers to come.

SNEAK PREVIEW -- PLANS FOR 1984!

Variety and verve....

The Professional touch....

Opportunity for talent in the region....an acting school....

In 1984 the Hangar Theatre Company will again offer four plays and one musical, with an emphasis on comedy. As usual this early in the season, we are still negotiating for rights to some plays and this may force changes. But we want you to know what we're planning and hoping to present.

William Goldman's _THE LION IN WINTER_ will open the season on June 26th. The final performance of our last play, Lindsay and Crouse's Pulitzer Prize-winning comedy _STATE OF THE UNION_, will be on Labor Day. Both plays are witty discourses on national and family politics, giving us a chance to compare 12th century Europe with 20th century America.

Our third and fourth shows had their original productions at the Actors Theatre of Louisville; both later enjoyed great success on Broadway.

John Pielmeir's _AGNES OF GOD_ is a powerful modern-day drama about faith, values and the mind. It is based on actual events that took place in the Upstate New York area.

Hazlehurst, Mississippi is the setting for _CRIMES OF THE HEART_, by Beth Hinley, which won not only the Pulitzer Prize but also the New York Drama Critics Award in 1981. This play is a funhouse of accelerating, rollicking misfortune which will keep you laughing as three southern sisters deal with a 'real bad day.'

To the tune of 'You Gotta Have Heart,' 'Whatever Lola Wants,' and many other high-spirited musical numbers, our second offering follows the humorous adventures of the Devil, his side-kick Lola and an avid Washington Senator's fan who hope to keep those _DAMN YANKEES_ from winning the pennant.

This mix of comedy, music, politics, religion and baseball promises our audience a season that is both entertaining and provocative. We look forward with excitement to opening night.

Another exciting event in 1984 is the start of a school of theatre arts. Our successful "Next Generation" program is being transformed into a first rate training school for young adults. We have high hopes that this will develop into a very successful activity.

Obviously there is much to be done in the months ahead. Money will be needed....and commitment, and faith.

Please invest in the Hangar today. We need you!

Sincerely,

Dave

David Allee, President

P.S. We need you because moral and financial support will be especially important this year. I urge you to use the enclosed form and become a Hangar member, today! Thank you.

Mailing List Of 900 Nets $3,000

This letter solicited support for a women's cultural arts organization. The results of the pledge campaign begun by this letter netted $3,000 from a mailing list of 900.

First impression. A full yet uncrowded page indicates clarity and seriousness.

Underlining. People who skim this letter will see key words: "tax-deductability," "pledge," "vital," and "facts."

Text. The tone is confident. The reader is reminded that Amber Moon has "brightened our lives" and that "every individual's contribution (is) important."

Facts. The letter gives exact figures: funds needed, deadline, amount already raised, and plans for raising more.

Closing. The last paragraph makes broad, positive references to Amber Moon. It affirms the donor while requesting a "responsible" reply. The final plea is accented with underlining, and adds a "please."

Return Envelope. A separate return envelope includes: suggestions for donation amounts, whether future billing is desired, and name, address, and phone number. Donors are also informed they will be publicly thanked.

Follow-up. Second letters were sent, with specific text targeted to out-of-town listings and former donors.

Repeat performance. The entire process is repeated annually.

Paula Wood

Amber Moon Productions, Inc.
P.O. Box 22096 • Lexington, Kentucky 40522 • 606/252-3110
A non-profit women's cultural arts organization serving Central Kentucky

March 20, 1983

Dear Friend:

Last year at this time, the Pledge Committee of Amber Moon was formed as part of an overall fundraising drive aimed at rejuvenating and sustaining an organization that has worked for the past six years to enrich and brighten all our lives. Amber Moon continues to shine for all of us and continues to need our support and energy. Thus, once again, we are asking you to make a financial contribution in the form of a pledge, renewable each year. This tax deductible pledge, no matter what the amount, is vital to the continued well being and growth of Amber Moon.

Why is every individual's contribution so important? Quite simply, without private donations of funds, Amber Moon, a totally non-profit organization, cannot continue to produce women's cultural arts events. In the present economic climate, with fewer and fewer dollars being allocated at the state and national levels for organizations such as Amber Moon, these organizations must rely increasingly on the generosity and commitment of the community they serve.

Let's review the facts. Amber Moon Productions, Inc. was conceived in 1977 by and for women, the child of imagination and caring. From the beginning, Amber Moon has served as a cultural beacon light to illuminate our lives. But, this light will grow dim unless we raise $5800.00 by September 1, 1983. This amount must be raised in order to qualify for the Governor's Challenge Grant. This grant will provide .25 dollar for every dollar we raise.

As of March 1, 1983 our fundraising efforts have realized $1600.00. In addition, we hope to raise $500.00 at the Casino in April and another $300.00 at the Yard Sale in May. Both of these events are aimed at "fun raising" as well, so we invite you all to attend and enjoy. Information concerning these events will be provided in our next newsletter.

These events, however, cannot generate all the funds we need. We must raise at least $3400.00 from private donations. Therefore, we are asking that every woman and man who has been entertained, enlightened and uplifted by Amber Moon events in the past six years take responsibility to nurture and encourage Amber Moon. Please fill out and return the enclosed pledge envelope. Help to keep the beacon bright and strong.

Sincerely,

Laura Van Slyke
Laverne Zabielski

Pledge Committee
Amber Moon Productions, Inc.

Environmental Agencies

Missing Raccoon Makes The Difference

The enclosed letter is used by our membership department in an effort to retrieve "hard-core non-renewers." Our dues-paying members receive an annual renewal notice and two follow-up reminders, if required. Members who fail to respond to our routine renewal requests are "raccooned." Our response rate to the raccoon letter is 30%.

We are fortunate in having a very talented photographer, Gerrie Reichard. Her photographs are taken at the Wildlife Center, of animals under our care. Her award-winning raccoon photo is one of the most popular items we sell at our fund-raising events. It becomes doubly appealing when the sad-looking orphan is separated from his brothers and sisters. Virtually everyone who responds to this letter writes a note commenting about the lonely little raccoon in the lower right-hand corner. Many people cut him out and literally put him back in the picture. One respondent colored a red bow around his neck.

The text, designed to be short and simple, probably has relatively little to do with the success of the letter. It merely underscores the message: the importance of the individual to overall picture.

Alice C. Katzung

Editor's Note: This entry was awarded Second Prize.

WE MISS YOU !!!

Dear Former Member of the Wildlife Center:

We are sorry you dropped out of the Wildlife Center picture. We miss you, and we need you. Each individual member is of vital importance to us, a fact which many people do not realize. Each year more and more animals are brought to us for care and our costs continue to rise. If we are to survive we must have support from you and others in the community who understand the importance of helping our wildlife. Please come back.

Sincerely,

Alice C. Katzung
Executive Director

Please put me back in the picture. Enclosed is my check for membership in the Marin Wildlife Center.

__Individual $12.50
__Family 15.00
__Contributing 25.00
__Supporting 50.00
__Sustaining $100.00
__Patron 250.00
__Benefactor 500.00 & up

Name:______________________________

Address:______________________________

____

Marin Wildlife Center P.O. Box 957 San Rafael, CA 94915

"Well Written And Homespun"

Organization: The Nature Conservancy is a national, land conservation group seeking to protect endangered species by saving their habitats. The national organization solicits the same local membership base twice each year using sophisticated computer mailings. The state chapters must compete with national for its local operating funds.

Target Group: 5,538 past donors, all Maine Chapter Conservancy members.

Results: 497 Gifts, 9% response rate. $22,943 total, $46.16 average gift. This includes 3 stock gifts totalling $4,500 from three former $10-$50 donors.

Basic Approach: The reader is quickly hooked by an interesting, personal tale. Each paragraph is carefully varied. No paragraph exceeds 7 lines. An easy to read typeface (Letter Gothic) is used. These things make the letter pleasing to the eye and easily readable.

The sentences are kept short. The story is woven to relate to the interest of the reader and the Conservancy. It is detailed enough to provide a clear vision in the mind's eye, yet not sound phony. (It happens to be a true story, but it is most important that it **sound** true.)

It is written in a conversational, storytelling style. When necessary to make the story flow, "proper" english and grammar is ignored.

The last paragraph on the first page is short and compelling. It **must** be read. The reader then just has to know **what** is so depressing about an otherwise upbeat story. The reader then hears the answer and gets to the point of this letter. This is where the pitch is made.

The end of the letter creates a sense of urgency. It calls for a quick response. "Like milking the cows, it won't wait."

This letter worked well because it was well written and homespun. It is clearly and intentionally local. Unlike the often impersonal, sophisticated nature of a national organization, this letter is homegrown. It doesn't start off talking about the world going to hell in a handbasket, it talks about my grandmother in the personal and intimate tones likely to be spoken to a good friend.

John W. Jensen

THE NATURE CONSERVANCY

MAINE CHAPTER

20 Federal Street, Brunswick, Maine 04011
(207) 729-5181

May 13, 1983

Dear Maine Chapter Member:

I always enjoyed hearing Grammie Jensen tell me about her childhood in Windham. She was born and raised on a family farm in this rural town of several hundred people.

Windham was 10 or 12 miles from Portland and made up of woods, streams and farms and not much else. There was much to do starting at 4 a.m. when she and a few of her brothers got up to milk the cows and start the rest of the morning chores. As you can imagine, milking the cows and most of the other morning chores simply could not wait.

Every other Saturday morning, Grammie would get up a bit earlier than usual. After the cows were milked, she would help her dad load the wagon, hitch up the team of horses and start on the several hour trip to the Portland farmer's market. Portland was the big city. It was a trip she anxiously awaited because Portland was so new--so different in her eyes. You can well imagine the excitment of a young farm girl in this situation.

This was a chance to explore a bit, learn of things new and unexplained and, if the farmer's market went well, she might even be given a special treat from one of the downtown stores.

I'm sure this was a common story back around the turn of the century. But to a city boy like me, it was always fascinating. The detail, the richness, the remembered childhood enthusiasm--all were so unlike my world of today.

I saw my grandparents and heard these stories when they again were living in Windham a few years ago. You see, the world of my grandmother's past lived only until I reached the door to her house.

Once I went through the door, I was back to the Windham of today.....a Windham which is now a sizable suburban town of 10,000 or 12,000 people rushing about. A town where farms are now very much the exception. A town that Grammie Jensen thought would never change.

It also was a bit depressing to me.

NATIONAL OFFICE, 1800 N. Kent Street, Arlington, VA 22209, (703) 841-5300

Windham has changed, along with the rest of the country. It is exceptional only because it occurred so fast and because I was able to learn of how it was before the "progress" of modern development brought its inevitable pressures to bear.

I can't even say that it was bad (except of course to my grandmother). People did (and still do) need places to live. A certain amount of development clearly is inevitable.

All that we can do is focus some of that development elsewhere.

We (as individuals, governments or groups like The Nature Conservancy) really cannot determine where development is going to take place--that is simply not practical in this world of ours--rather, we can only decide on those places that should not be changed or developed.

And even this will occur only if we care enough to make decisions and act. Just talking about the changes will accomplish little. It may make you feel better to talk about the problem, but those who are changing Maine's landscape are doing a lot more than talking--you can bet on that.

Like the way that Grammie Jensen simply could not put off milking the cows, you and I simply must do what has to be done--and do it now. Help save those vital and dynamic patches of wildlands. Allow your grandchildren and mine to be able to see these areas--not just hear us talk about how wonderful they were back in the 1980's.

Make out a check--$100, $200, $500 or whatever--and send it to the Maine Chapter.

Make your gift as large as you can. It's tax deductible, so it will save you a bit when you settle up with Uncle Sam next April. But more importantly, it will save a big bit of what you and I really love about Maine.

Like milking the cows, it won't wait. So please sit down, write out a check, slip it in the reply envelope and put it on the kitchen table. Then make sure to take it with you when you go out.

Thank you for being one of those willing to accept the responsibility for playing a vital role in The Nature Conservancy's work in Maine.

Cordially,

John W. Jensen
Executive Director

Aaron And President Combine For Success

The "Aaron letter," three days in production, went in September 1983 to 643 donors to a Spring 1983 appeal, which had requested funds to hire horticulture students for our Summer Internship Program. After talking with the 1983 Interns, I decide Aaron Danielson's sincere thankfulness for his opportunity to work at the Society's River Farm translated perfectly into a thank-you letter to the donors who had made his employment possible.

I wrote the letter; Aaron signed it; we put his photo in the corner, and typed the letter to look like something a student might produce on his own typewriter. Our President wrote an accompanying letter, his second thank-you to these donors; it included a soft appeal for support for the 1984 Program.

To minimize costs, we substituted a specially-marked business reply envelope for the typical contribution card. The total mailing cost $253.60. It generated $4936.20 from 70 donors—a 10.9% response, with an average gift of $70.52. It also generated good will: most donors included warmly supportive letters with their second contributions to the Program. This letter's success supports my belief that personal, strongly-written, inexpensively produced appeals can be real direct mail winners for non-profit organizations.

Thank you for considering our "Aaron letter," the most profitable thank-you letter we have sent!

Connie Clark

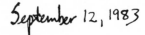

September 12, 1983

Dear Member of the American Horticultural Society:

I want to thank you for giving me a job this summer as an Intern at AHS headquarters, River Farm.

If it hadn't been for contributions from you and other AHS members, the Society could not have hired me, and I would have missed a very special opportunity.

At the beginning of the summer, I had a job with a moving company which paid much more than the AHS Internship. But when I heard about the Internship, I applied anyway. And even though I need the money I earn each summer for college expenses, I quit the high-paying job to work here at River Farm.

My friends asked me why I did this. Well, I have loved plants since I was in fourth grade, and I am majoring in biology, with an emphasis in plant science, at North Park College in Chicago.

But I never had much formal training with plants till this summer. Now, I've done a little of everything -- general maintenance, dividing iris, clearing undergrowth for the new Woodland Walk, pruning roses, watering (at 6:00 a.m.) to keep the whole place from turning brown during a prolonged hot, dry spell.

The work has been hard but exciting. I feel I have more than just theory behind me now as I go on to learn more about horticulture. I might not have been this philosophical about my summer job on some 98° days, but looking back, I know nothing could replace the experience.

I'm especially interested in plant propagation now, and I've put in some beds at home with roses I've started from cuttings. I'm also trying my hand at rooting boxwood. I'll be leaving my new garden to go back to Chicago soon, but at least the feeling of accomplishment will go with me, even if the plants won't.

I want you to know that I really appreciate the contribution you made to the Summer Internship Project. Being an Intern taught me things I wouldn't have learned otherwise. It changed my life. And, speaking for the other 1983 Interns as well as for myself, I thank you very much.

Sincerely,

Aaron K Danielson

Aaron Danielson

THE AMERICAN HORTICULTURAL SOCIETY
MOUNT VERNON, VIRGINIA 22121

September 12, 1983

Dear Friend,

I think Aaron Danielson's letter says just about everything that needs to be said about our Internship Project, but I want to add my personal note of thanks.

The future of the Project was shaky this spring. I faced the prospect of cancelling it, though I knew how valuable it could be. Your contribution, along with others from Society members, pulled us through, and we were able to bring five Interns aboard for the summer of 1983.

This year's Interns learned a great deal and helped immensely with the maintenance of our 25 acres. Their youthful energy also made it possible for us to start projects, like our Woodland Walk, which a lack of manpower had delayed.

It has been richly rewarding to see these young people learn the all-important lessons you learn only by getting tired and dirty in the hot sun. I feel the Society has met its goal -- though only a few Interns were trained this year -- of enhancing horticultural education in this country.

Naturally I want to see the Project going strong next year. In fact, I'd like to double the number of Interns at River Farm in 1984. To do so, and to avoid an emergency appeal letter like the one I sent this spring, I am planning now for 1984's program.

I hope you will consider extending your generosity again for next year's crop of young horticulturists. Your gift to this Project will prevent any last-minute scramble for funds next spring, and will continue the wonderful tradition you have helped start here at River Farm.

Please take a moment to re-read Aaron's letter. You have given him and his fellow Interns a unique opportunity to learn and grow. Then please use the self-addressed envelope I have enclosed to say "Yes" to 1984's Internship Project.

Once again, thank you very much for your support of the American Horticultural Society -- and thanks for making a summer of hands-on horticulture possible for Aaron Danielson.

Sincerely,

Edward N. Dane

Edward N. Dane

END/cd

A Mailing To 800 Raises $20,000

This was only the second fund appeal for our small land conservation organization; with it we raised a third of our 1984 operating budget. Of its 800 recipients, almost 100 responded, with gifts totalling just under $20,000.

When I wrote the letter, I focussed on the following:

> using a personal, informal style suitable for our small western community (and, incidentally, the style of the letter's signer).
>
> establishing both a sense of opportunity and urgency.
>
> building credibility for an organization which had been active for only two years.
>
> creating for the reader a sense of involvement, as well as personal community pride and responsibility.

It seems to have been just the right approach.

Jean Hocker

JACKSON HOLE LAND TRUST

November, 1983

"What fate does the next decade hold for the large open ranches that give Jackson Hole its character today?

'It's very simple,' said one rancher, 'they will all be covered with houses.'"

Jackson Hole News
3 January 1980

Looking around our magnificent valley, I think that rancher was wrong. Sure, in the four years of this decade houses have certainly replaced haymeadows, and roads and buildings have pre-empted important wildlife habitat.

But I still see grazing Herefords and sweeping hayfields giving Jackson Hole its special character; I still see open and natural areas harboring moose, deer, eagles and cutthroats on private lands. I still see the unique balance that sets Jackson Hole apart from the Vails and Aspens.

If I didn't, I wouldn't be writing to you today. I know you're as grateful as I am that houses haven't marched across meadows or along rivers and streams quite as quickly as the rancher predicted. Because it tells me that the landowners--and all of us who care about this place--still have some time to take other choices, practical choices for protecting ranchland and open space.

Photo: Phil Hooker

POST OFFICE BOX 2897 JACKSON WYOMING 83001 PHONE 307-733-4707

2

The Land Trust is in the business of offering those choices. And, as you'll see by reading the enclosed brochure, we're beginning to do it pretty well. Do we think we'll turn back the clock to the Jackson Hole of days gone by? No, of course not. Do we think we're making an important difference? You bet we do!

But we really need your help. Two years ago, we asked for financial assistance to set our land protection programs in motion. The response was unexpectedly generous, demonstrating that people really do care about this place. We vowed to prove ourselves and our programs before asking for money again, even if it meant stretching our resources pretty thin.

Now we feel comfortable and confident about asking for your donation--comfortable in knowing that we've already protected some key lands of Jackson Hole and are on the verge of protecting much much more--confident that there are large numbers of people like you who don't want to see the rancher's prophecy fulfilled.

I know you get a lot of requests for donations--especially at this time of year. Only you can decide where to put your charitable dollars.

I can tell you, though, that few gifts will provide more tangible results, or an outcome that will affect you more directly, than a donation to the Land Trust. Your gift for 1984 will help us offer a greater variety of protection opportunities to more people, for more land in this remarkable valley of ours.

Please, won't you write a check today? Naturally I hope you'll make it as generous as you can. But a check of any size will help. We'll be very grateful for your assistance. And I think you'll feel good about your investment in Jackson Hole.

Many thanks.

Sincerely,

Vincent R. Lee
President

P.S. Even since the enclosed information sheet was printed, we've been asked to help with two more exciting projects totalling more than 700 acres--one along the Snake River, one along the Fish Creek Road. We hope to have details on these for you soon!

V.R.L.

Letter Stresses Giving Opportunities

This direct mail letter and accompanying giving catalog are the best we have ever created for obtaining donations of cash and gifts. Since its inception nine months ago we have received over $20,000 in cash donations, over $10,000 in equipment, and a foundation grant of $36,000 to construct a beaver pond boardwalk—all on an investment of $700.

A designer donated camera ready artwork, and a printer provided mechanicals and the use of his printing press free of charge. This gave us 10,000 copies to provide over the counter to park visitors or to direct mail recipients.

A mailing list of 4,000 individuals, businesses, institutions and foundations was prepared over a four-month period to ensure that distribution coincided with media publicity.

The letter—and giving catalog—work because they appeal to people with emotional ties to Rocky Mountain National Park. The array of proposed gifts are as small as $.10 to preserve one square foot of land. Hence even children can donate and measure the extent of their gift.

From this one effort we expect donations will eventually exceed $100,000.

Glen Kaye

RESTORING ROCKY
A GUIDE TO GIVING

Dear Friend of Rocky:

Since its inception in 1915, Rocky Mountain National Park has been a daily delight for millions of people. It's a source of inspiration. It brings peace of mind. It offers inspiration and learning.

The character of Rocky is stunning--so much so that 3,000,000 visits are recorded each year, a tribute to the regard that Americans hold for this, the tenth national park in the United States.

Its ecological values are equally significant, serving as a protected sample of one of the world's major ecosystem types.

Its values, educational, emotional and scientific, are inescapable. Yet for all its priceless character, Rocky needs help. Preservation is more than placing a fence around a preserve. Education is more than opening the gates. Providing both lasting protection and compatible use means an investment in equipment and services, and in a professional staff to accomplish the many things that parks mean.

In these days of constrained budgets, however, our goal is beyond our means. We therefore invite you to help us preserve and maintain Rocky Mountain National Park and serve the many visitors to this wonder of the world. Please review this gift catalog. It identifies tax deductible resource needs, the services, equipment and funding which are beyond our ability to provide. Your gift of any of these items can help make Rocky all it can be.

I welcome you as a partner in the preservation of Rocky Mountain National Park.

Sincerely,

James B. Thompson
Superintendent

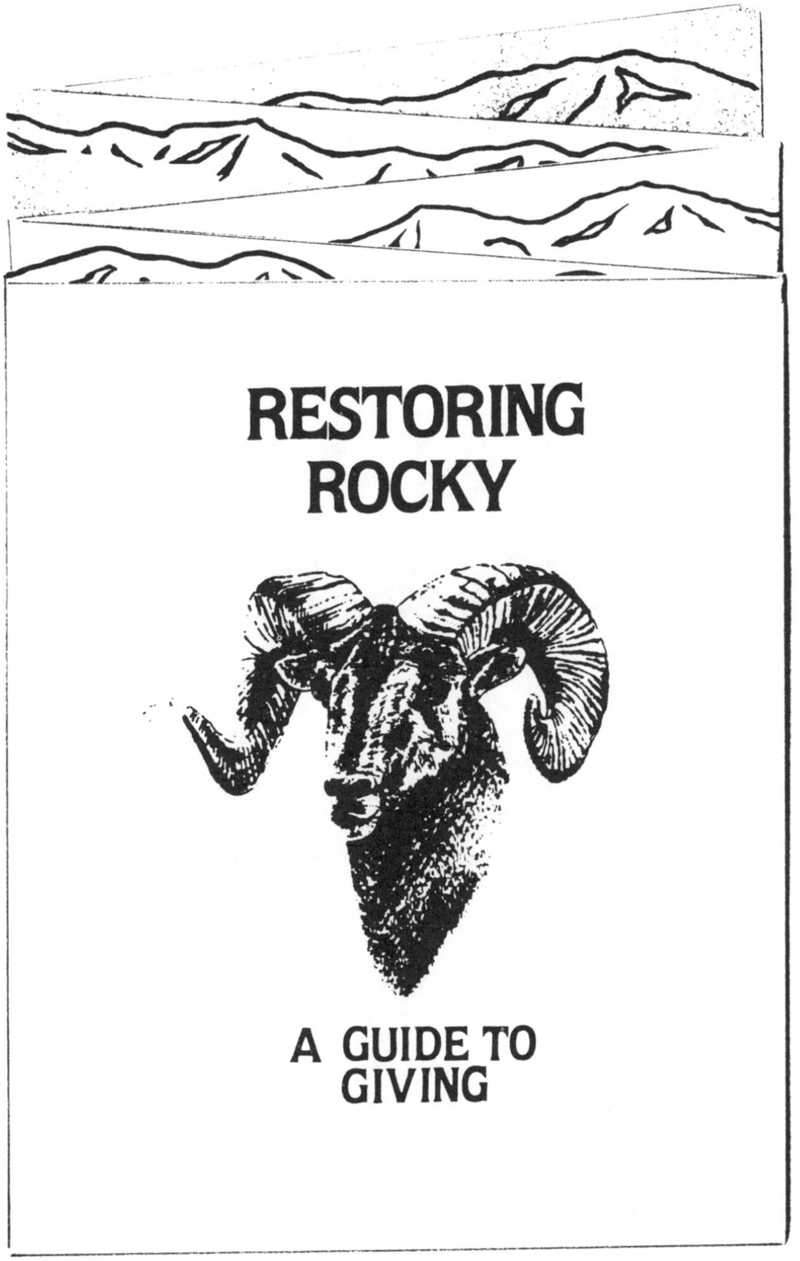
RESTORING
ROCKY
A GUIDE TO
GIVING

Religious and International Agencies, and Others

Best Response Ever

This entry of the Fellowship of Reconciliation was our best for fiscal year '83'-84. Titled, **The Day After,** this "Dear Friend" was mailed to 17,794 "house" names of members, contributors and subscribers to the FOR. The simply designed package was developed in response to the ABC television movie, "The Day After."

Statistically, this package was the best! Mailed in mid-October, 1983, just prior to the television film, the mailing has had a total response of 1665 for a 9.4% response rate; that's the highest of any mailing that year and since. As of June 18, 1984, $62,610 was raised for an average gift of $73.60. **The Day After** raised $3538 per thousand at a cost of $200 per thousand for nearly 18 times more money raised than spent per thousand. The mailing peaked in November and December with $25,351 and $22,553 respectively; another $11,300 was received in January with dollars still trailing in this month. The year-end mailing in December, to many of the same contributors also had typical excellent results.

The single page letter was unusual for FOR which normally sends a two-page letter. This majenta-colored package was one of the most attractive packages that year. Simple in design, the letter and return card coordinated the logo of the phoenix rising from the flames, a standard for FOR stationery at that time. The World Peace Prayer was appropriately coordinated with the message of the letter to raise the hope of those who viewed "The Day After." The premium offered, Muste's book on Gandhi, generated $6,300.

The package had some definite advanatages. First, its simplicity and attractiveness. Second, the benefit of an advance notice media event, consistent with the purpose of the organization. Third, the proximity toward the end of the calendar year may have been helpful. And, its singular success in FOR's direct mailing history has yet to be topped.

Jan Scott Hesbon

There is no way to peace...peace is the way

FELLOWSHIP OF RECONCILIATION. Box 271. Nyack, New York 10960 (914) 358-4601

October 1983

Dear Friend,

On Sunday, November 20, ABC-TV will show THE DAY AFTER, a 2-1/4 hour motion picture about what happens to a town in Kansas following a nuclear attack on the United States. Eighty million Americans are expected to see this prime-time event.

Polls have revealed that a majority of Americans believe that there will be a nuclear war in their lifetime. Children express fears that they will not live to adulthood. THE DAY AFTER may only deepen these feelings.

But it need not. Not if you know there is an alternative to helplessness and despair.

That alternative is what the FOR represents...affirming life and reaching out with hope and trust to people all over the world.

For nearly 70 years, the Fellowship of Reconciliation has stood <u>for</u> the power of truth and love to resolve conflict and to end war. Through its programs and campaigns, publications and speakers, local groups and regional gatherings, FOR has worked diligently for peace.

What will happen on THE DAY AFTER November 20? We urge you to make it a time for renewed action for peace.

To help FOR make an effective and widely known witness, please send a contribution today. In so doing you will be helping FOR's work against the Euromissiles and all nuclear weapons. You will also be helping to encourage the work of US-USSR Reconciliation, and the ongoing task of teaching the meaning of peace in schools, churches, and synagogues.

Thank you.

For the work of peace,

Richard Baggett Deats

Richard Baggett Deats
Executive Secretary

PS The World Peace Prayer postcard enclosed is sent to you as a reminder of the power of love. Please use it and share it with others.

We recognize the essential unity of all humanity and have joined together to explore the power of love and truth for resolving human conflict

—*From Statement of Purpose, The Fellowship of Reconciliation*

WORLD PEACE PRAYER
LEAD ME FROM DEATH
to LIFE, from FALSEHOOD to TRUTH
LEAD ME FROM DESPAIR
to HOPE, from FEAR to TRUST
LEAD ME FROM HATE
to LOVE, from WAR to PEACE
LET PEACE FILL OUR HEART,
OUR WORLD, OUR UNIVERSE.

"Appeal Pushed Us Over The Top"

This Appeal was sent to our donor list as well as to volunteer tutors (of the Laubach method). It was, without reservation, the best in terms of dollars raised and new donors obtained.

Personality and deep feelings radiate throughout the appeal.

Here we have a friendly, warm, and compassionate person (Dr. Bob Laubach) writing about his father in tender, loving words. The audience (donors) for the most part either knew Frank Lauback or heard him speak.

I tried—through Bob's words—to identify with the donor and the people receiving help.

The premiums, key chain and embedment, were icings on the cake and went over extremely well with donors.

Some of our board members felt the Appeal was not in good taste for such a noble person as Frank Laubach, but this vocal minority only convinced me I was on the correct path.

I was. The Appeal worked. Dollars helped the illiterate poor we serve. And—the board is still mad.

This Appeal pushed us over the top, making fiscal '83-'84 the greatest in the history of Laubach Literacy International.

Walter E. Brooks

Dr. Frank C. Laubach when he first went to the Philippines in 1915.

Frank C. Laubach "CENTURY CLUB"

February 16, 1984

But words are things, and a small drop of ink,
Falling like dew upon a thought, produces
That which make thousands, perhaps millions think.
George Gordon Byron—1778-1824

Dear Friend:

Like most important letters, this one began as a sheet of blank paper -- pure, lonely and frightening (to me).

Lord Byron's thoughts (above) put it all in focus, and so --

I am writing with something wonderful to share -- a golden opportunity for you to take an active role in the celebration of a man, an idea --

-- and to receive for your part, a special memorial gift(s) for your love and support for those less fortunate than you.

You see, 1984 would have marked the 100th birthday year of my father, Dr. Frank C. Laubach.

Perhaps you had met him, or heard him speak? Or knew him personally?

If so, this letter may bear deeper meaning for you.

To honor my father's 100th year, Laubach Literacy International's Board of Trustees, staff and volunteer leaders have established a special Frank C. Laubach "CENTURY CLUB" --

-- and invite you to join.

A brief mention of my father's life as an educator, author, teacher, missionary and inspiration, will set the stage for what I will suggest to you. First --

One must return to the Philippines of the '30s.

For it was then, thousands of miles away, the motto, "Each One Teach One," became the keystone of Dr. Frank's approach to adult illiteracy.

Among the illiterate people there, he saw the possibility of adult literacy education on a mass basis using inspired, volunteer teachers.

What he developed worked. . . .

Dr. Frank C. Laubach (circled) teaching New Guinea tribesmen in 1949.

Education of Millions!

The culmination of his efforts was the creation of the unique "Each One Teach One" method -- and the bringing to the forefront of man's awareness the terrible blight of illiteracy.

As a result, hundreds and thousands of volunteer Laubach tutors have been helping men and women learn at home and in remote corners of the world.

TODAY -- Laubach Literacy programs, an extension of my father's work, have resulted in the basic education of an estimated 60 million adults.

In his lifetime, my father was known throughout the world as one of the most unique and successful teachers of his day.

Through easy, effective materials,
he taught millions to read and think.

As I type this letter to you today, memories come back to me. "Long ago" seems to fade in and fade out.

And you must admit, "long ago" is a funny time of life.

Everything is fun if it's "long ago" ... and this wonderful, mystical, rose-colored hindsight is usually referred to by a most pedestrian word -- nostalgia.

However, I'll make my thoughts current.

Frank Charles Laubach left behind the faith that each of us can make a difference.

He made history. He belongs to history.

For his family, his friends and all who knew him, he was an eternal light in our life which still glows.

For tens of hundreds of thousands around the world who never met him, but who felt they knew him, his memory lives on, and his light reaches far into the darkest corners of human existance.

His spark still glows -- and I do not believe it will ever fade and die.

Prejudiced? Yes. For he is my father, and I love him.

Will you share your love for him in a different way?

Dr. Frank C. Laubach

Join the Frank C. Laubach "CENTURY CLUB" -- now!

By so doing, you will alter the lives of so many by improving the methods, materials, and Laubach service systems already in place in six countries.

And your gift -- large or small -- makes a mighty difference to those in need.

Remember -- every single dollar given to the "CENTURY CLUB" will go to support Laubach programs of your choice -- in Colombia, Panama, Mexico, India, Africa or the United States.

I feel you deserve a special remembrance for the charity you may show now -- as in the past.

But, I cannot give to you what you already have -- love for mankind -- hope for a better tomorrow -- faith in the work of Laubach Literacy International and its U.S. volunteer network, Laubach Literacy Action.

You know, your spirit of sacrifice and commitment humbles me.

So, I have been looking for the proper remembrance to send to you. . .

Some "memento of meaning" to express my honest love and admiration for the way you have supported the Laubach Literacy movement with your gifts and/or your volunteer activity.

Something of import -- not necessarily in dollar value -- has emerged which has meaning and significance. I hope you agree.

FRONT BACK
DIE STRUCK KEY TAG

Look at this—

Laubach Literacy has established four "CENTURY CLUB" groups and special commemorative gift(s) selected for each category:

For a gift of $25, you will receive a Registered Die Cut Key Tag and become a "CLUB" Member.

For a gift of $100, you will receive a Lucite Paperweight with an Embedment of a Die Struck Medallion and become a "CLUB" Charter Member.

FRONT

For a gift of $100 and your agreement to include Laubach Literacy International in your will, you will receive both the Key Tag and Paperweight and become a "CLUB" Life Member.

And ---

---for a pledge of $1,000, or a gift of $500 now, you become a Member of the exclusive "CIRCLE OF 100" ---

and will be honored........(please turn page)

BACK
LUCITE PAPERWEIGHT

Artist's rendition

⊢—— 2½ feet ——⊣

Capitol of the World's Literacy Movement—1320 Jamesville Avenue, Syracuse, NY.

And will be honored . . .

... by having your name or the name of a loved one -- along with the names of other "Circle of 100" donors -- engraved on a 2 1/2-foot, circular bronze plaque. *You will also receive the Key Chain & Paperweight,*

The plaque will be installed in the "Lobby of Honor" at Laubach Literacy International headquarters in Syracuse, NY.

Your most generous deed and name will be there in a special and honored setting.

Everyone who sees the gleaming plaque will know of your selfless sacrifice to help illiterate adults served by Laubach Literacy programs.

Our dollar goal for the Century Club is $100,000. ← *April 30 deadline!*

I assure you that every dollar raised for the "CENTURY CLUB" will be used not only to increase the quantity of Laubach services, but to improve the quality of the Laubach programs available.

But -- dear friends -- whatever size gift you send, it will be prudently spent to upgrade Laubach Literacy services -- and to honor, in a special way, the man who opened the minds of millions.

Thank you for helping those who cannot read or write.

I am turning to you today because you have always been there when I really needed you. Now I really need your support more than ever before.

Not for me. Nor Laubach Literacy. But for those we both serve -- God's children who are mired in poverty and ignorance. Please help. So very, very many need you.

Sincerely,

Dr. Bob Laubach

Robert S. Laubach, Chairman
Board of Trustees
Laubach Literacy International

PS: Names of all donors -- regardless of the size of the gift -- will be recorded in a handsome and permanent "CENTURY CLUB" Register Book.

'Hobo' Letter Meets Dual Goal Challenge

In the Spring of 1983 the Humane Society of Seminole County Florida was faced with a do-or-die challenge to match a $50,000 grant, which would assure its reaching a $125,000 building fund goal for a badly needed animal shelter. Numerous approaches had been attempted—special events,a few major individual and corporate donations, etc.—but a final push was needed to meet the challenge grant deadline just four months away.

Besides immediate income needed to meet the grant challenge, the small humane society also needed to begin building a solid membership base. The goal, therefore, was two-fold—a difficult assignment for a single direct mail appeal letter.

The result was what I call the "Hobo" letter, which was directed to both prospective and existing members.

As developed for the society, the letter's primary appeal was an emotional true-to-life story about a little dog, which spelled out the society's purposes and services, and why the public's help was needed.

The inexpensive die cut (punch-out) involvement device—which helped the recipient to change the little dog's picture, by moving it from a negative to a positive environment—was undoubtedly a significant factor in giving response.

The dollar matching challenge grant provided a strong secondary emphasis in the original "Hobo" letter. Less emotional, but appealing to those of a more pragmatic turn of mind.

A combined letter-reply slip format was selected because it helped tie together copy and graphics, with the puppy tracks used to "lead" the reader to the all important reply coupon. The leading process actually begins with the outer envelope; the teaser copy being the actual beginning of the "Hobo" story.

Did it work? Here are the stats. You be the judge.

Letters were mailed to a selected list of 38,500 prospects and an ill-defined list of 2,700 current and expired members. The total in-mail cost (including postage) was $9,978.00. Gross dollar returns totaled $25,284.00, providing a net income of $15,306 . . . a return on investment of $2.53 for each dollar spent, plus adding 635 new members to society rolls.

If there are lessons to be learned from this "dual goal" appeal effort, I feel they are, primarily:

DON'T hesitate to use emotional copy and graphics;

DO everything you can to **involve** the reader . . . including use of involvement devices when appropriate;

DON'T make it hard for your reader to grasp just what you want him/her to do . . . lead him/her by logical, interrelated copy and graphics from (1) openinig your envelope and (2) reading your message to (3) filling out the reply coupon, and . . .

DO spell out **benefits** (not features) of your cause, and provide compelling reasons to make a gift **now**.

Carroll L. Scott

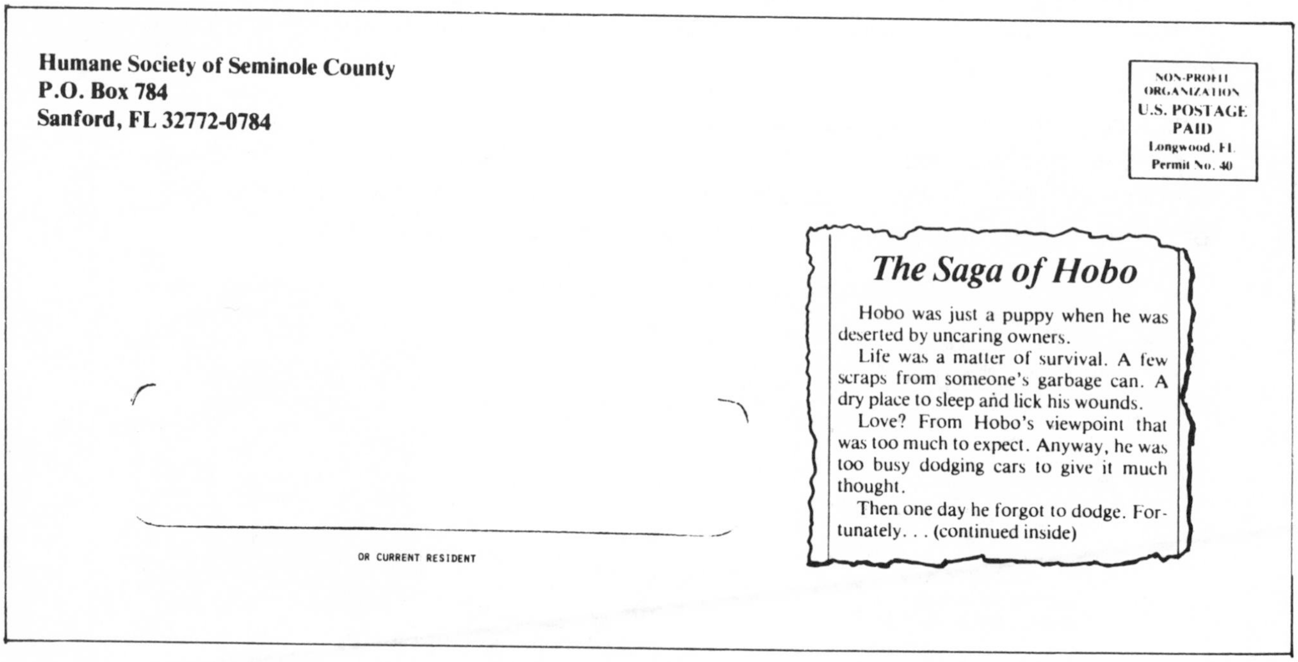

Humane Society of Seminole County
P.O. Box 784
Sanford, FL 32772-0784

NON-PROFIT
ORGANIZATION
U.S. POSTAGE
PAID
Longwood, FL
Permit No. 40

OR CURRENT RESIDENT

The Saga of Hobo

Hobo was just a puppy when he was deserted by uncaring owners.

Life was a matter of survival. A few scraps from someone's garbage can. A dry place to sleep and lick his wounds.

Love? From Hobo's viewpoint that was too much to expect. Anyway, he was too busy dodging cars to give it much thought.

Then one day he forgot to dodge. Fortunately. . . (continued inside)

Want to Save Hurt, Hungry, Homeless Animals? *Accept This Challenge* And Start With Hobo. *(just punch out circle, and follow his tracks)*

Dear Friend;

Fortunately for Hobo, someone cared enough to bring him to the tiny animal shelter of the Humane Society of Seminole County, located on East 25th St. in Sanford.

Treated by a veterinarian, and nursed back to health by the shelter's small staff and many willing volunteers, Hobo learned for the first time what it meant to be clean, healthy, well-fed-- and loved.

Yes, Hobo's true-to-life story has a happy ending. And, in time, I'm sure he will be adopted into a real home. But what about the thousands of other unloved and frequently abused creatures in our community?

How Will They Survive and Find Caring Homes?

That's why I've come to you now. To explain how you can make the difference in the lives of many animals like Hobo-- by accepting an important challenge from the Society.

The Humane Society of Seminole County has been meeting animal welfare needs throughout our community since 1973. We are a non-profit, non-tax supported organization dedicated to the relief of pain and suffering of all abused and injured animals.

Besides emergency transport, veterinary care and adoptions, we place emphasis on low-cost spay and neuter services, as a primary solution to animal over-population; humane education; investigation of cruelty cases; lost and found-- and a host of other animal/people related services.

Only available shelter space, facilities and operating funds dictate how many animals we can serve, and how long we can care for them.

And that depends on folks like you. . . who care enough to help.

The Needs are Urgent and Growing

As our community continues to grow at an unprecedented rate, our most pressing need is space. To meet this need, we have stepped out on faith by breaking ground for a much enlarged and centrally located animal shelter in the Five Points area of the county. However, we have only until this fall to complete the shelter, or relinquish the tract on which it is to be located.

But There's Good News As Well

Many hundreds of caring folks have already joined in this effort. And only recently we received a "challenge" grant offer that can assure the much needed new shelter!

The Challenge — And What It Means

The Edyth Bush Charitable Foundation has approved a grant of $50,000 if we match it with new donations of a like amount by August 1st.

This means your gift NOW will be effectively DOUBLED by this generous offer!

The attached reply form further explains how you can share in this exciting challenge, and help fill this critical need. Just follow Hobo's tracks. . .

Then please say, "YES, I accept the challenge," by sending your tax deductible contribution today.

Sincerely yours,

Helen Wolk

Helen Wolk, President
Humane Society of Seminole County

P.S. If your contribution to this critical need is $25 or more, I'd like to personally send you our Society's Humane Certificate of Appreciation.

(Detach and mail Today)

This is your ADVANCE RECEIPT

For your convenience, you may fill in amount of your contribution, detach and retain this stub for your files. It will serve for tax deduction purposes, subject to verification.

Date__________

Amount $__________

Check #__________

Contribution to HUMANE SOCIETY OF SEMINOLE COUNTY

Thank You!

(Detach and Save)

Yes, I accept the challenge!

Here is my tax deductible gift of ( )$100 ( )$50 ( )$25 ( )$15 ( )Other $__________ to help build a new shelter to care for the hurt, hungry and homeless animals of our community. If my contribution is $25 or more, I will receive the Society's **HUMANE CERTIFICATE OF APPRECIATION.** Also, I understand that my gift **NOW** will be effectively **DOUBLED** by the Challenge Grant!

If you are not presently a member, your gift of $5 or more entitles you to a subscription to our bi-monthly newsletter.

Please Note: Your name and address label is attached to the back of the enclosed reply envelope. Please do not deface label. If corrections are needed, please provide information below.

NAME ____________________

ADDRESS ____________________

CITY__________ STATE______ ZIP ______

With your help, we can find him a REAL home.

Results Four Times Greater Than Before

Eastern European Mission distributes Bibles in Russia and Communist Eastern Europe. EEM found a "golden opportunity" in the crisis in Poland in 1981.

The public news media was focusing daily on the Polish crisis. EEM capitalized on heightened public awareness of Poland to spotlight its efforts in Poland during the fall of 1981. Instead of competing with information from the new media, we selected an interesting and current theme on which to base EEM's fall appeal.

The fall mailings were computer generated, impact-printed, one-page, monarch-size, personalized letters. The letters to significant donors who had made gifts of $100 or more, and to donor churches were auto-typed on word processing equipment and sent in closed faced envelopes with first class stamps. Each received a personalized gift reply form and business reply envelope. A similar follow-up appeal was sent six weeks later to non-respondents.

Results: The total dollars raised from 3,500 donors and 40,000 prospects exceeded $250,000.00. The results were four times those raised by similar mailings the fall before when Poland wasn't so prominent. Donors responded at a 20.6 percent rate at a phenomenal cost of only 8 cents per dollar raised. Non-donors produced a dramatic 5.9 percent response rate at a cost of 18 cents for dollar raised.

One key to the success of the mailings was the 30 day time limit imposed because of threatening weather conditions. Capitalization, underlining, and dramatic writing heighten the appeal. Specific goals, broken down into donor-sized segments of $3.00, $7.00 and $10.00, helped make it easy for the donor to see what his gift would accomplish. By tying the appeal to current events, the donor was given a chance to become a part of the news.

David Oakley

EASTERN EUROPEAN MISSION

CHURCH OF CHRIST ON BAMMEL ROAD
P. O. BOX 90755 • HOUSTON, TEXAS 77090

October 23, 1981

URGENT

Mr. David A. Sampleperson, Jr.
NLT Computer Services Corporation
National Life Center
Nashville, Tennessee 37250

Dear David:

Praise God -- we have a golden opportunity!

I've just learned the atheistic-controlled government of Poland will permit us to distribute the new translation of the Polish Bible INSIDE the country legally!

This extraordinary opportunity is made possible thanks to the $500,000 our Churches of Christ sent to help feed needy Poles. In response, the government is dropping its barriers and allowing us to import copies of a new Polish Bible, put out by the Austrian Bible Society.

But that's not all. The Polish leaders have set no restriction of the NUMBER. In other words, EEM can flood the country with as many copies as we can to print!

But -- here's the challenge. We can only take Bibles into Poland for a period of THIRTY DAYS. This means we must act fast to get across the borders just as many Bibles as we possibly can. Our goal is to send 50,000 Bibles and New Testaments.

We've carefully computed the cost and $7 pays for a complete copy of the Bible -- $3 for a single New Testament portion. You can easily see what your gift of $10, $17, $21, or more will mean in this effort. Please, write out your check for as much as you can and RUSH it in the enclosed envelope TODAY. Such an opportunity may never come again!

Sincerely,

Dave Oakley

David Oakley
Director, U.S. Operations

P.S. Remember, the Polish winter weather gives us only 30 days to bring Bibles. So do hurry your gift!

Best Direct Mail Package Ever

MIVA America considers its latest direct mail package to be the best it's ever created because:

It uses word pictures. Readers can "see" images of women carrying heavy bundles and American missionaries struggling through mud, fording rivers and picking their way along mountain paths.

It asks for the money that's needed. Transportation is expensive—often, a missionary's biggest expense—and the food and medicine you can buy with a few dollars is useless if you can't get it to the people who are hungry and dying.

It has a large number of elements to pique a reader's interest. There's a letter, an i.d. sticker, a reply card (with a message from Mario Andretti, a MIVA America board member and auto racing veteran), a brochure with photos and a return envelope.

It offers choices. You can contribute by using your credit card or writing a check. You can write for more information—the list of vehicles provided by MIVA America in 1983. Or even if you don't do anything else, you can keep the i.d. sticker. And display it.

One segment of the mailing was extremely successful: as of August 10, 1984, it had pulled in nearly twice the dollars it needed to. We had judged the minimum acceptable income per thousand to be $1,403.85. The actual income per thousand, as of that time, was $2,269.23. And contributions are still coming in.

Other segments of the mailing did not meet our projections in terms of total income, but there's a postive side there, too: in general, the average dollar gift met **or exceeded** our projections.

For those reasons we think the package is a good one.

Alan Janesch

Missionary Vehicle Association, Inc.

HOW MANY GROCERIES
CAN YOU CARRY HOME ON YOUR HEAD?

Dear Friend in Christ:

A strange question perhaps! But all around the world -- in developing countries -- the amount of food and medicine that a mother can buy for her family depends on how much she can carry home on her head. How much shopping for you and your family -- at your food store or drug store -- could you do without a car to take your goods home? Not much.

And yet, Americans take missionaries' travels for granted. We picture them going from village to village in a picturesque far-off country. But do you ever imagine them struggling through mud, wading across river beds, picking their way up and down miles of goat paths ... or feel their remorse when they finally arrive at a village hut with life-saving supplies only to find that the sick person died?

The outlying and far-flung villages of a missionary's flock may be scattered twenty to two hundred miles apart. Not far on an American road map, or on American roads, to be sure. But in bad weather and in rough terrain, it is a horribly long distance, especially on foot. And it becomes an impossible distance when trying to carry forty or fifty pounds of food and medical supplies.

Transportation is Needed

Year after year, good people like yourself have assisted the foreign missions. Your generosity has brought critical supplies, health, and hope to millions of God's poorest. But that is not enough. It is the missionary who has to deliver the nutritional foodstuffs ... the medical supplies ... and who must minister to the sick that you have helped with your contributions. But oftentimes the missionary entrusted with your gifts can't reach the people who need them the most, because he or she doesn't have the necessary means of transportation.

MIVA America, through our Christopher League, is working with missionaries all over the world to help them buy the necessary means of transportation -- 4-wheel drives, pick-up trucks, jeeps, and even oxcarts and burros. Any dependable vehicle can become a "bearer of Christ" and help a missionary deliver lifegiving food and medicine, and the message of God's love. And every vehicle greatly multiplies the number of poor and suffering people each missionary is able to teach and serve.

How You Can Help

It's true that $3 or $5 a month will buy a great deal of food and medicine for overseas missions. But it's equally true that $5 won't buy much of a jeep. We are appealing not only to your generosity ... but we are asking you to make a real sacrifice ... to make it possible for us to buy these precious "bearers of Christ".

If you're an average American, you drive about 12,000 miles a year. We are asking you to offer a penny a mile to God's work ... a contribution of $10 a month -- every month -- in thanksgiving for your safe passage. We are asking you to remember the hazardous, dangerous, and dreadful conditions that the messengers of

MIVA America 1326 Perry Street N.E. Washington, D.C. [illegible]

God face every day while you ride comfortably in your car back and forth to work, on vacation, and to visit your friends and family.

"Almost a Miracle"

MIVA was founded in 1972 to provide vehicles to American missionaries. The vehicles listed below are "almost a miracle." Each of these missionaries has been pledged half the funds to buy an essential vehicle. MIVA currently lacks the ability to match these pledges, but with your help, wė can help these missionaries achieve their "miracles":

* Father Oliver Branchesi of Nairobi, Kenya needs a pickup ($10,000) to shuttle among his medical dispensary, maternity clinic, home for the elderly, and 12 seminaries.

* Sister Antoinette Cusimano, ASC, in Liberia needs a car so she and her sister companion, a nurse, can minister to the spiritual and physical needs of the surrounding villages. Her order has promised to match MIVA's grant but we need $6,900.

* Brother Brendan Flahive of Chonnam, South Korea needs a 4-wheel drive Jeep ($10,000) "ambulance" to transport tuberculosis and cancer patients to his medical clinic and to deliver medicines to those bedridden in rural areas.

The transportation needs of missionaries are much greater than just the examples above and your sacrifice and generosity are greatly needed.

Benefits to Contributors

Sustaining Members of the Christopher League -- monthly contributors -- will be remembered daily in the Masses and prayers of the missionaries who receive help. As a Sustaining Member you will receive a beautiful acknowledgement card, and a quarterly summary of the activities and grants of MIVA America. You'll know where and how your money is being used.

Every contributor, regardless of the amount of their offering, will be remembered in the prayers of missionaries all over the world.

It's simple to give

Please complete the enclosed contribution form and return it to us. You may use your charge card to take the hassle out of your monthly gift. We'll simply have your card billed each month for the amount you indicate -- no check writing, no stamps, no bills. And any time that you want to discontinue your contribution -- for any reason -- just call us or drop us a note and we will stop the contribution.

Naturally, if you prefer to send us a check, please do so. Whether you can contribute or not, please affix the enclosed identification badge to the dashboard or sun visor of your car and remember you are in the prayers of our missionaries.

Thank you for your sacrifice.

Yours with the poor,

Phil De Rea M.S.C.

Father Philip De Rea, MSC

P.S. If you would like a list of the vehicles provided by MIVA America in 1983, please mark the request box on your contribution form.

I'm Mario Andretti, and I want to talk to you about speed and danger.

We Americans have made some pretty remarkable contributions to transportation in this world, and we use speed to test them out. In practice, in time trials, and on the racetrack I risk my life to test new and experimental vehicles and to provide thrills to thousands of spectators. For me, fast vehicles and danger are a way of life.

But for thousands of even more courageous men and women -- America's foreign missionaries -- any vehicle can save a life. Every day they work to bring medicine, food, education, and hope to millions of people less fortunate than us. For them, speed -- or the lack of it -- means how much food can be delivered in a day, how fast sick people can be moved to the nearest clinic or hospital, and how many lives can be saved.

MIVA America is an organization working to meet this critical need for transportation in the developing world. It gets down to the basics. It provides American missionaries with cars, vans, trucks, jeeps, motorcycles, and even bicycles and oxcarts.

As an active member of MIVA America's Board of Directors, I know first-hand that with your help, we can continue to make some pretty remarkable contributions to transportation in the Third World.

Please send your contribution to MIVA today.

Yours,

Mario Andretti

Played Up Current Tense And "You"

We received a 5.98% response (average gift just over $35) from 20,216 solicitations. The response does not include many follow-up gifts which we received through our receipting process. The letter was folded once (requiring a large envelope) perhaps making it appealing to open and easy to read. The paper quality also added to readability.

The photos and the script support each other equally. We were able to keep it all to one page (two sides). We obviously played up the "You" and emphasized the present tense encouraging the readers to see themselves as currently involved.

It was also stressed that the reader/donor contribution makes possible the commitment of other financial and non-financial ingredients which help the projects to be successful. In other words, the donor doesn't feel that he/she is doing all the work.

I also believe that establishing the authority for our solicitation (see the post script style of note referring to our denomination's endorsement) was also helpful to establish credibility with the reader.

We needed $29,915.47 of income to keep faith with our 85/15 proportion for charitable purposes versus administrative costs. We received $42,345.91 (again, not counting follow-up gifts through the receipting process).

Cameron Stuart

Outreach International

P.O. BOX 223 • INDEPENDENCE, MO 64051 • (USA)

Do you know what you make possible through OUTREACH?

Dennis Labayen (at left in upper left photo) is an expert in community development and the new Field Director for **Outreach** (as described in the *Saints Herald*, September 15, 1982 issue). Dennis knows about Third World poverty. He grew up in the Philippines and works with the rural poor there. He has also worked in Bangladesh and amongst the poor in other countries. Dennis knows that what the poor person thinks makes a big difference in what the poor person can do. A community development project quickly becomes worthless if the poor think of the project as foreign to their interests and culture. Dennis listens. And then Dennis knows what **we** can do to work **with** the poor. **You** make this possible.

The facility pictured in the top right photo is a great cause for celebration. Located in the rural Philippines, the Shaw Training Center is used to train Filipinos in food production, marketing and other pertinent skills. Villagers are taught by Filipinos in a building designed and constructed by Filipinos and even located in a Filipino rice paddy. The Shaw Family Foundation was happy to provide the funds for this project partly because of the dedication of so many others who are providing regular financial support to **Outreach**. In other words, **you** make this possible.

In the lower right photo the man being confirmed a member of the RLDS Church has been for seven years the agricultural leader in the CORD project in the Philippines. Charles Neff (at right) and Kisuke Sekine (at left) have been CORD officers for some time. They are also ministers and Apostles in the RLDS Church. A Filipino, a Japanese and an American are brought together and pictured here in this commitment to Christ because of a physical ministry through community development. **You** make this possible.

The bottom left photo shows a mother and child in Honduras. The child has maramus, a severe form of malnutrition. They are members of the RLDS Church. Their pastor, using information obtained from Dennis Labayen in a seminar funded by **Outreach**, worked out a locally appropriate health and nutrition program with the family of the sick child. **You** make this possible.

The Lord has given all of us physical and spiritual resources. He wants us to use those resources to take dominion over disease, poverty and oppression. It is possible. And **Outreach** is a powerful tool in this ministry of possibility.

Please give to **Outreach**. We renew our pledge that at least 85% of unrestricted charitable donations will be applied to projects.

Yours in His service,

OUTREACH INTERNATIONAL

Cameron Stuart

Cameron Stuart
Executive Director

Outreach is the sole authorized fund raiser to support human resource development among church members and church jurisdictions. —*Saints Herald*, August 1, 1979, p. 34.

OUTREACH

A MINISTRY OF POSSIBILITY THROUGH

All photos were taken in 1982.

3 From '76

To complete this book we are reprinting the three top prize winning letters—with their commentaries—from the first edition of the book published in 1976. In this instance you are indeed reading the best of the best.

Expressing Genuine Feeling

Memorial Hospital of Bedford County is located in a rural area in the mountains of Pennsylvania. Patient care here is very personal. People are people, not ailments or numbers. Very often, the patient is someone you know or who is close to someone you know.

Dying is also a very personal thing. We know not all patients get well. Families don't expect miracles. But when a loved one dies and a hospital takes the time to write a personal word of condolence, it means a lot to the family members.

Very often we have received replies thanking us for caring. We don't mention memorial funds in our letter, that's not the time. But the letter of condolence leaves the family with a good feeling toward the hospital and some day—maybe years from now, maybe tomorrow—that same family may be asked to contribute to a building fund or to an Auxiliary project and the little time it took to say "we're sorry" can "pay off" in response to a hospital need.

Our letter is sincere. Hospital employees feel the loss when a patient dies. Every letter is an original and it comes from all of us.

Patricia Morgart

MEMORIAL HOSPITAL OF BEDFORD COUNTY
Route One, Everett, Pennsylvania 15537

Telephone: (814) 623-6161

James C. Vreeland
Director

Date

Mr. John Doe
Any Street
Any Town, U.S.A.

Dear Mr. Doe,

Probably a letter expressing sorrow and regret at the passing of a loved one is the most difficult of all to write. I know it is for me.

There is so little one can say that can alleviate the sorrow or dull the pain caused by the loss of a loved one.

When the Supreme Architect of the Universe calls one of us, the most modern and scientific medical care and treatment is of no avail.

On behalf of Memorial Hospital of Bedford County, the Board of Trustees, the Medical Staff and the entire staff of employees, please allow me to express to you and to the members of your family, our sincere sorrow at your loss.

Most sincerely,

James C. Vreeland,
Director

JCV:pm

A Successful LYBUNT Letter

Our December 15, 1972 LYBUNT letter (enclosed) was addressed to approximately 600 alumni who had contributed to the annual fund the prior calendar year but had not repeated their gift by the end of the first week of December of 1972. The letter was mailed first class, a warranted variation from our policy of non-profit rate mailings used in large mailings. Our standard reply envelope accompanied the letter.

By the end of the second week of January, over 500 of these alumni had responded with their gift. Additionally, we received more good humored accompanying notes that ever before, alluding to the fact, as one put it, that they "didn't want to be a lybunt forever or a lycanthrope ever."

The calendar year fund drive went over the top with this mailing, and we have since used the opening lines to similar advantage in mailings to special gift club donors, parents, and friends. A very successful letter thus has had an extended life—with multiplied results.

Brendon L. Haggerty

DIRECTOR OF ALUMNI RELATIONS 202 529-6000

THE CATHOLIC
UNIVERSITY
OF AMERICA
WASHINGTON D.C. 20017

Dear Alumnus:

Did you know that you are a LYBUNT? (Thankfully, a LYBUNT has nothing to do with a lycanthrope, the closest word in the dictionary; but happily is a creature for whom every development officer has a special place in his heart). Every alumni fund office maintains a list of the special friends of the University who donate to the fund each year. At the close of the year it often takes only a reminder to those who made a contribution Last Year BUt Not This to renew the valued assistance of concerned alumni. If our mail has crossed or a tired computer is running behind on recording, please attribute our repetition to enthusiasm and forgive us!

This year has been a peak year in many respects, as we have reported in the new University publication "Envoy." 1972 has already seen a charter membership of 50 in the newly inaugurated President's Club of $1000.00 donors. Total alumni contributions already challenge last year's high of $150,000, and the welcome support of our LYBUNT friends bodes the greatest year in the history of The Catholic University of America alumni fund when the total response is tallied after December 31.

Will you give now as you so generously did in 1971? While the future of our University is bright with promise, much depends on the generosity of CUA alumni as we gear for a growth and a preeminence of which we can all be justly proud.

A wish for the blessings of the Christmas season upon you and yours joins this at once grateful and hopeful communication.

Sincerely,

Vincent P. Walter, Jr.
Director, Alumni Relations

"Love Is Green"

Enclosed is a copy of the best direct mail letter the Children's Home Society of Minnesota has ever created and its follow-up letter as well.

"Love is Green" was the campaign theme of Children's Home Society of Minnesota's 1974 membership drive. Instead of doing a letter from our president, we decided to try a new approach—a letter written by our clients, the homeless children who are waiting in foster care. The Society needed a hard-sell approach for this year's campaign since membership revenue had been relatively constant for two years. The theme "Love is Green" was the hard-sell approach we needed but it was softened with the pre-school writing style and the fact that it was written by those who would benefit from increased membership gifts. The copy made effective use of a play on color words and their meanings. The message was simple and direct—a membership renewal will bring the children love through adoptive placement.

The cost of this campaign was downright cheap and the results have been CHSM's best ever.

Ellen Johnson

A gentle reminder

LOVE IS GREEN.

Please send us some love!

By putting a little **GREEN** in your membership envelope

Your **GREEN** will help us get to Loving Moms + Dads

Your **GREEN** will also keep CHSM out of the RED.

Come On Now, **Us kids** are counting on **YOU**!

WE'RE BLUE!

'CUZ YOU HAVEN'T SENT US ANY GREEN $!

Your green will help us get to waiting Moms + Dads,

And will chase away our blues!

PLEASE RENEW YOUR CHSM MEMBERSHIP!

Love, Us Kids

About The Publisher

Public Service Materials Center was established in 1967 to meet a need for useful and informative materials relating to fund raising development. In addition to **A Treasury of Successful Appeal Letters,** publications currently available from PSMC include the following:

THE CORPORATE FUND RAISING DIRECTORY—1985-86 EDITION
Now accurate up-to-date information is available on the huge $4 billion grant-making programs of America's top corporations. Here you can find out who to approach at each corporation, primary areas of giving, typical grants, special insights and other vital information $79.50

HOW TO HAVE A SUCCESSFUL CAREER IN FUND RAISING
By Dr. Randall P. Harrison
This is the first book—practical in every detail—that tells you how to get to the top in your fund raising career. And because money isn't everything, it also tells you how to get the greatest possible degree of emotional gratification from your work $27.00

HOW TO RAISE TOP DOLLARS FROM SPECIAL EVENTS

By Mira Sheerin

Encyclopedic in scope, Mira Sheerin's new book will remain the definitive guide to successful special events for many years to come. No detail that can help you have better and more financially rewarding special events is left uncovered..... $24.00

FUND RAISING BY FORMULA—STEPS TO MAKE PEOPLE GIVE

By Dr. Randall P. Harrison

This revolutionary new book by one of America's leading research psychologists not only tells you why people and organizations give, but provides a step-by-step process by which you can increase the level of support your institution receives in almost every important area $19.95

SUCCESSFUL BUSINESS VENTURES FOR NONPROFIT ORGANIZATIONS

By Charles Cagnon

In today's difficult times, many nonprofit agencies are trying to **earn** money as well as raise it. This is the best book yet printed on this important subject..... $16.75

GRANT MAKING CORPORATIONS THAT PUBLISH GUIDELINES

Now—for the first time—here is a listing, with addresses and telephone numbers, of 241 grant making corporations that publish guidelines and will send them to you on request $8.95

RAISING FUNDS FROM AMERICA'S 2,000,000 OVERLOOKED CORPORATIONS

By Aldo C. Podesta

Finally, there is a book that tells you what to do to raise dollars, not only from America's giant corporations, but also from the thousands of corporations in your own back yard. And it comes at a time when everyone agrees that corporate fund raising is about to take a quantum leap forward $24.00

WHERE AMERICA'S LARGE FOUNDATIONS MAKE THEIR GRANTS (1983-84 Edition)

This is the most complete representative record ever published giving the specifics of grant-making by leading foundations in this country. It includes over 650 foundations in every part of the nation, most with assets of $10 million or more $44.50

NEW WAYS TO SUCCEED WITH FOUNDATIONS —A GUIDE FOR THE REAGAN YEARS
By Joseph Dermer
Joseph Dermer has written an important new book designed to help non-profit organizations not only survive the Reagan years, but to grow stronger through increased foundation support. It is the first book that provides specific strategies for differing non-profit institutions to undertake at this time in approaching foundations $19.50

THE COMPLETE GUIDE TO CORPORATE FUND RAISING
Edited by Joseph Dermer and Stephen Wertheimer
To begin with, this book is a superb technical manual. You will never again wonder how or what you should do to win corporate support. But that's just the beginning. Special sections of the book tell you how to raise corporate funds if you are a university or hospital, a cultural institution, an advocacy organization, social service agency, or just a smaller institution $16.75

THE 1983-84 SURVEY OF GRANT MAKING FOUNDATIONS
The all new 1983-84 Survey of Grant-Making Foundations contains vital information nowhere else available. Listed are nearly 1,000 foundations, all with assets of over $1,000,000 or grants of more than $100,000, with such information as the best time of year to approach them, whether they make general operating grants, whether they will give you an appointment, to whom you should write, and whether they expect to increase grants $15.95

500 WAYS FOR SMALL CHARITIES TO RAISE MONEY
By Phillip T. Drotning
This is the newest and most important book yet published on fund raising for the smaller agency—where perhaps no more than one person is responsible for the full gamut of fund raising and public relations $16.00

HOW TO WRITE SUCCESSFUL FOUNDATIONS PRESENTATIONS
By Joseph Dermer
Here are step-by-step instructions in writing successful foundation presentations, together with full examples of grant-winning proposals. Subjects covered include writing appointment letters, presentations for general operating funds, special projects, capital funds as well as others $11.50

HOW TO GET GOVERMENT GRANTS
By Philip Des Marais
Finally, there is a book describing in simple, straightforward language how your institution should go about securing governmental grants—from your first organizational step to the final accounting of how your institution spent the funds $15.50

THE COMPLETE FUND RAISING GUIDE
By Howard R. Mirkin
Drawing on a rich, varied background, one of America's leading fund raisers spells out the specifics of conducting virtually every kind of fund raising campaign including raising funds from government, business and labor, foundations and the general public $17.50

FOUNDATIONS THAT SEND THEIR ANNUAL REPORT—BOOK TWO
Here are the names and addresses of over 600 foundations (assets of over $1,000,000 or grants of over $100,000) that will send you their annual report on request at no charge $8.95

THE NEW HOW TO RAISE FUNDS FROM FOUNDATIONS
By Joseph Dermer
Written in practical, down-to-earth language, this manual covers all aspects of foundation fund raising from getting appointments to writing proposals. It is now recognized as a classic in its field $11.50

HOW TO WRITE SUCCESSFUL CORPORATE APPEALS —WITH FULL EXAMPLES
By James P. Sinclair
A leading authority on corporate fund raising opens his files to reveal all his secrets of writing successful appeals to corporations—and provides you with an extraordinary range of grant-winning samples $19.75